Satisfied

ALYSSA JOY BETHKE

Satisfied

Finding Hope, Joy, and Contentment Right Where You Are

Worthy
Hachette Book Group
1290 Avenue of the Americas, New York, NY 10104
worthypublishing.com
twitter.com/worthypub

First Edition: May 2021

Worthy is a division of Hachette Book Group, Inc. The Worthy name and logo are trademarks of Hachette Book Group, Inc.

The publisher is not responsible for websites (or their content) that are not owned by the publisher.

The Hachette Speakers Bureau provides a wide range of authors for speaking events. To find out more, go to www.hachettespeakersbureau.com or call (866) 376-6591.

Vegetable garden photograph on page 90 by iStock | SbytovaMN.
Gardenia bush photograph on page 34 by Shutterstock | Lapha.R.
All other photographs are by Jenna Strubhar Photography.

Unless otherwise noted, Scripture quotations are taken from the Holy Bible, English Standard Version®, ESV®. Copyright © 2001 by Crossway, a publishing ministry of Good News Publishers. Used by permission. All rights reserved. | Scripture quotations marked (NIV) New International Version®, NIV®. Copyright © 1973, 1978, 1984, 2011 by Biblica, Inc.™ Used by permission of Zondervan. All rights reserved worldwide. www.zondervan.com. The "NIV" and "New International Version" are trademarks registered in the United States Patent and Trademark Office by Biblica, Inc.™ | Scripture quotations marked (NLT) are taken from the Holy Bible, New Living Translation, copyright © 1996, 2004, 2015 by Tyndale House Foundation. Used by permission of Tyndale House Publishers, Inc., Carol Stream, Illinois 60188. All rights reserved. | Scripture quotations marked (MSG) are taken from THE MESSAGE, copyright © 1993, 2002, 2018 by Eugene H. Peterson. Used by permission of NavPress. All rights reserved. Represented by Tyndale House Publishers, Inc.

Print book interior design by Laura Klynstra.

Library of Congress Cataloging-in-Publication Data has been applied for.

ISBNs: 978-1-5460-3404-9 (hardcover); 978-1-5460-3406-3 (ebook)

Printed in China

APS

10 9 8 7 6 5 4 3 2 1

To the women I hold so dear to my heart

May we be a generation who finds deep satisfaction in the Lord alone,

joy in all the daily, mundane, ordinary ways of life,

where he is beckoning us to see his beauty and joy and to have his peace.

CONTENTS

Part I

Chapter 1

LONGINGS MET

How lovely is your dwelling place,

O Lord of hosts!

My soul longs, yes, faints

for the courts of the Lord;

my heart and flesh sing for joy

to the living God.

PSALM 84:1–2

I looked around the circle of women who had gathered on my patio this early morning. With candlelight dancing around, I noticed some looked ready for the day, while others literally rolled out of bed. (A couple of my friends later admitted to sleeping in their bras so they wouldn't even have to dress in the morning. *Yes, girl!*) I was honestly surprised they all showed up. After all, it was only 6 a.m. and many had babies who had probably kept them up all night, and I wasn't serving coffee or muffins. But here they were, ready to pray.

With the timer on my phone set for an hour, we prayed and cried and repented and gave thanks and worshipped and breathed and shared silence and uplifted each other. It was one of the most beautiful gatherings I've ever been a part of. Sleepy-eyed and pajama-wearing, we had shown up and the Lord met us on that patio. Not only was it sweet to hear my friends talk with Jesus and hear what was heavy on their hearts, but I heard Jesus calling me to lay down all that I had been grasping at for so long. To release all the pressures, fear, and anxiety. To let go of control and trust his mighty, capable hands. While I've prayed through those things a lot, there was something about saying it out loud with other women there to hear and pray with me. Tears, mixed with yesterday's mascara, rolled down my cheeks. I was so relieved to hand it all over to God.

Getting to this place wasn't easy, though. Have you ever prayed for a new thing—a new job, a baby, a husband, an opportunity, a move, a home—and the Lord said yes and made a way and gave you the very thing you've desired, but then afterward, your life was still hard? You still had challenges, and it wasn't all that you thought it would be. And even if you know it's good for your soul or your family, it's still not easy. There are still some frustrations about receiving what you wanted, or it's still lacking in some way, or it has challenges, or it still leaves you holding on for dear life. It doesn't fully satisfy you. Or it simply wasn't what you were expecting. It didn't meet all your ideals.

I prayed for years that God would bless me with a husband, and he so graciously gave me Jeff. But marriage reveals your true heart, and it is hard work to continually choose the other person and become one. When Jeff and I got married, I quit my job so I could travel with him. Sounds dreamy, right? He was gone all the time back then, and I simply wanted to be with him. It was good for our marriage and we made incredible memories, but with it came a lot of identity issues I had to work through. Those issues were compounded by getting married, then quitting my job, then having a baby, and then trying to figure out where I fit into this new life. I began praying that we could move back to Maui, a place where my soul felt at home and where the Lord had brought me a lot of healing and freedom. And, miraculously, God made a way for us to make that move! But it didn't play out the way I thought it would.

Our main reason for moving to Maui was to be in community with other young families, something that we didn't have in Washington. Since I had lived there previously, I figured finding friendships and community would be easy and was something that would happen quickly. And yet that first year was one of the loneliest I had ever experienced. Jeff was traveling a lot since he had made previous plans before our move, so it took longer to dive into relationships here. But many of my friends I had previously known had moved away, and my time to connect with old friends who remained was more limited because now I had a family. Plus, making new friends as a mom is kinda tricky. (Shoot, making new friends as an adult is hard!) Sometimes it felt like I was dating all over again! I would meet someone at a park, exchange numbers, and then try to plan a playdate. But would we actually connect in the few minutes we had to talk between interruptions and potty breaks? And would our kids get along well with each other?

One day I was sitting in my room while my oldest daughter, Kinsley, took her afternoon nap. Tears ran down my cheeks onto my open Bible. *Drop, drop, drop.* I felt so lonely and rejected. I know no one was actually rejecting me, but here it was, months after we'd moved to Maui, and I still didn't have any friends. Not ones I felt comfortable enough with to call on a whim and hang out with, not ones to really pour my heart out to, not ones to be in my daily life. I had tried multiple times to get together with another mom, but it just didn't seem to be working. I would finally gather up enough courage to text someone, only to have them respond with a "sorry, can't today" or not respond until much later. Finding mom friends with the same napping schedule was hard during that season. And having dinner with friends was rarer since Jeff was gone a lot. After hearing a friend say she couldn't get together, not out of spite at all, but simply because it didn't work with their schedule, I would go into a deep hole for a week, until I got the courage to ask someone else, most of the time coming up empty-handed again.

My lonely heart ached. I thought God had made a way for us to move to Maui so we could have community, but why was that not happening? Why was this so painful? There were tons of young families here, and yet I was still alone every day. Then I remembered what my friend Leslie had said: "Alyssa, let your loneliness push you into God's presence."

Loneliness is so painful; yet, God redeems it. He uses it to draw us into his presence. Either I could see my loneliness as a great wound and sulk in it, or I could let it lead me to the presence of Jesus. I wrote in my Bible, "Lord, may I long to dwell with you, and to dwell in your courts, more than anything else." No matter how lonely I was, or how long the loneliness would last; no matter if I made a friend the next day, or if it took years to

develop roots, my God was with me always, and he longed for me to dwell with him. It's there that I would find a true friend, a true comfort, a true counselor.

Sometimes, I desperately ached for Jesus to be with me. Wouldn't it be so much more comforting if he could just appear and physically hold me? I found myself crying out to him, "Father, I wish you could physically be here with me right now. I wish you could physically hold me and I could cry in your arms." What comfort and peace I would find.

But every time I have cried that to him, he's reminded me that his Spirit is with me always—my helper, comforter, and counselor. Jesus has also provided a tangible love through my family and my friends. Arms open wide. A hug. A note of encouragement. Flowers. A listening ear.

When we look at Scripture, we know God's heart is one of great love, compassion, and grace. His heart longs for us to come to him. He knows the condition of our hearts, he knows every thought we think, he knows that we are but dust, and he wants to work on our behalf. His arms are always open to us.

When we let down our walls, we can find healing and freedom. Perhaps we will always be on a journey of learning vulnerability. One step at a time we let down our guards, let go of the fear, and rely on him more. Jesus whispers, "Come. Lay your burden at my feet, let me carry it for you. Tell me your true thoughts, the lies you're holding on to, and ask me for help." Most likely we will still have to face the things we dread regardless of our prayers, but laying those things down before him allows us to feel hope. Suddenly, we have the courage to do the hard things, the strength to press forward, the peace in the storm, the hope in the devastation. Our hearts are transformed as we pray, because we get to know him and learn to trust him more and more. Prayer is not necessarily about us changing God's heart, but rather, him changing ours.

I desperately longed for girlfriends, for mom friends, for friends to invite over for dinner or to hang out at the beach with. I was heavy-laden with fear, rejection, and loneliness. But as I continued to dwell with him and pour out my heart, he spoke to me about how he never leaves me. He gave me the courage to keep trying. To keep asking for friends. To put together Bible studies, small groups, parties—anything to meet and connect with women. He gave me hope as I waited.

Throughout all of my longings, Jesus' answers to my prayers have drawn me closer to him. They've brought healing and growth. They've left me on my knees crying out to the Lord because I always need him. Why does that surprise me? Yes, I stand amazed at his goodness to me and his blessings, but I also kneel humbly, thankful that he is not done working in me. That he is faithful to bring to completion the good work he began in me (see Phil. 1:6); and that in every season, he is at work in me. Perhaps that is the true

answer to prayer. To be brought close to his side, his arm wrapped around my shoulder as he steps into the new thing with me, and gives me another opportunity to trust and rely on him, even after he has fulfilled my longing.

Eventually I did make friends. Bianca was my first. She's hilarious, fiercely loves her people, and is a safe place. She pursued me and was always up for hanging out when I would ask her. Then Jess moved here with her adorable family, and she felt like the sister I never had. Sarah was next. She has become the person I process with, SOS text with, and do battle with. Those three besties didn't happen overnight, but over four years. And in between those three, I have developed sweet friendships with a handful of other women whom I adore. Women I laugh with, pray with, exchange long texts with. They're my family's people who bring us homemade bread at 8 p.m. because they're thinking of us, who say yes to girl nights and prayer meetings and Bible studies. They're my family's people who come to our house when tsunamis or fires make it unsafe to remain at their homes, people who are with us for every holiday dinner, who come to the hospital to meet our babies, who do garage sales together and shop my closets, and who bring their kids to our co-ops and host baby showers together.

I have gained the courage to invite women into my life only as I seek God and let him speak to me. He gives me visions of gatherings and puts people on my heart and will move in me to ask someone to gather together. Every time I hear his voice and do it (shakily

sometimes!), I'm surprised at their response. An immediate yes! An "I've been praying for this!"; "This is exactly what we need"; or "I was just thinking the same thing."

The only way I could keep trying, keep asking, was to change my thinking. Instead of thinking, "I need friends. Who will want me?" I had to start saying to myself, "Who can I be a friend to? Who needs some encouragement?" I had to be okay with being the pursuer, whether they responded or not. If I always am to be the one asking or leading, that's okay because I'm imitating Christ and how he pursues us always. I can pursue because he pursues me.

Perhaps the longing isn't so much about the move or job change or school or husband or child or friend or answered prayer, but rather about receiving the gift of turning toward Jesus and learning a new way to surrender and trust. To know him better. To learn to rely on him in a way that we hadn't before. And to once again find him to be trustworthy. I think it can be easy to subtly believe that when we receive whatever we're praying for, we'll be satisfied or complete or comfortable or happy. And there is some truth there. When God answers a prayer, it is such a gift. And our faith is built stronger. I think of the proverb that says, "Hope deferred makes the heart sick, but a longing fulfilled is a tree of life" (Prov. 13:12 NIV).

Perhaps the real gift is the time we spend beforehand, asking, waiting, watching, and being with Jesus. And then the time after, of continuing to praise him, thank him, and ask him for wisdom and help, again. Another waiting. Of learning a new dance. A new rhythm. A new cadence. God gives such good gifts, but the sweetest thing of all is that *we get God*. He is our gift. And he will be with us in every longing, during the long wait, and after. No matter what transition we may be facing, that truth will never change. He is with us always. He is with us as we kneel on the floor and ask him, again. As we crawl into our closet with tears in our eyes, crying out to him, and asking, again. He will be with us as we enter the new season, the new thing he has miraculously done, when we find

our steps to be shaky and our expectations not quite what we thought. As we encounter hard days, still; longings unfulfilled, still. Ideals not quite so ideal. Even in the yeses we still need God, and the good news is that he always gives all of himself, always. He is the same God in the waiting as in the receiving.

Often we look to some change to be the answer, and even if it's a wise decision, a good move, something that is healthy, we forget that we're still human, living in a fallen world. There will still be things that are challenging. We are still in need of a Savior, and we need him every day. To rely on him. To look to him to be our joy, for him to fill us up and be the answer. It's like there are two layers—the first layer being that this is a wise decision and for the best; and the second, deeper layer being that we must remember that God is the only One who will ever fully satisfy our longing souls. No matter what season we're in, which gift we receive, we still need Jesus. And he is ultimately the best and truest gift.

Now looking around that prayer circle, I felt so bonded with these women because it was as if we were fighting together, on one another's teams, linked arm in arm in prayer. I'm reminded how it's worth it to seek God, to form that habit of prayer. It doesn't come naturally to me, but it is something that I need to actively pursue. He doesn't expect me to know all the depths of my heart, to speak eloquently, or to even know what I'm saying half the time. He just wants me to come to him. And sometimes, it is coming with others. Being willing to be honest. Honest about my fears, my hurts, my desires. To confess with others. To petition with others' "um-hmms" and "amens" next to me. We are not alone in our longings and desires. We are not forsaken in our sins and wrongs. We are welcomed into the arms of the Father and into the community of believers. Just as we are.

Hope is ours regardless of if we ever receive our longing on this side of heaven, because we have Hope himself. And let us not forget that this life on earth is short. The Kingdom of heaven is coming, and in eternity with Jesus, we will never want for anything again. Longings will pass away, because we will have all that we ever wanted in him. He satisfies us here on earth, but in eternity our satisfaction will never wane. We will always be filled up, our faith will become sight, and we will dwell in his light and goodness forever. We won't hope for things anymore, because our true hope will be made our reality. Hope is ours today, and as we continue to live in this tension of waiting and hoping, we can rejoice that one day every desire of ours will be fulfilled. But for today, in your waiting and wading through, have hope friends. For Hope himself is yours.

Chapter 2

HOLY MOMENTS

Make it your goal to live a quiet life, minding your own
business and working with your hands.

1 THESSALONIANS 4:11 NLT

In an age of being seen, of having followers, getting likes, and being noticed, being unseen can seem foreign and certainly not welcome. With a push of a button, we can enter into so many lives—of our friends and of those we admire. To see their stories of what they had for lunch, what their days consist of; to see their gatherings, homes, homeschooling, and dates with their husbands. We get tiny glimpses into it all, whether they are close or we've never met them before. We post too. We fill people in on our child's new funny thing, what new project we're working on, and what our day has consisted of.

I love it. Truly. I've made friends online—good friends whom I hold in my heart and walk life with and who understand me in a way that others don't. I love that we can have a community there when sometimes our lives do not afford many girl-gatherings or heart-to-hearts in person. I often feel encouraged as a mom, that I'm not alone, that some homeschool days look chaotic for them, too, that they're also wearing a messy bun and the same shirt from yesterday. That they are giving their lives to love their kids and be intentional with them, and integrating their families into their callings.

Somewhere along the way, though, we have lost the art of getting away with God, to be with him alone, to seek his face and not everyone else's. I have found myself going to social media when I'm feeling down, when the stress of the day is overwhelming, when I don't know what the next step is. I wonder, "What would so-and-so do in this situation?" When I feel empty inside, unsatisfied, disheartened, or sad, I try to fill the emptiness with beautiful images, or to enter someone else's world for a bit.

Have I lost the art of silence? Of quiet? Of hearing his voice over it all? How much am I missing out on what *he* wants to show me? Oh, it can seem like I'm missing out on a whole lot of things when I scroll through others' dreamy pictures or see their fun-filled vacations on their Instastories. But what am I sacrificing for the sake of catching up on everyone else's lives?

I often use the time after the kids are in bed to catch up, but sometimes that means suddenly an hour and a half has passed and all I've done is scroll. Which I love. But I know when it's from habit, and when I'm numbing out, and when I could choose to do something more filling. Now, please hear me: I'm not saying don't get on your phone. Sometimes it's absolutely what we need, but we know our hearts. We know when we need to implement a new habit, put off a not-so-filling one, or put something off because it's keeping us from becoming our best selves. Oftentimes, I think if we asked Jesus, "How do you want me to spend this hour, this time, this night?" we'd be surprised by what he says. Sometimes it may be to rest, or maybe it'd be something totally different where he persuades us to get away and hear from him.

Personally, I found myself wasting so much time on that little screen, and getting wrapped up in so many other voices, that I lost my own, as well as the voice of the One who had been speaking over me for my entire life. I suddenly didn't know who I was, what I should be standing for, or what I should be sharing. I didn't stop to talk to God, or to hear what he wanted to tell me about a certain situation, but instead I quickly clicked a button to let all the noise in, to find a quick answer, to try to solve problems on my own.

I felt God saying, "Alyssa, put down your phone for a bit. Look at the life I've given you. Look at these gifts I've given you. Come to me, and let me speak over you. Let me give you a voice, as I speak to you. Let me be the One to direct you in the way you should go. Let me tell you what is going on in your child's heart; let me nudge you in what to pray for about that relationship; let me whisper to you my love and affection. Come find your rest and truth in me. Let me be your healer, your escape, your rescue. Let me carry all your burdens."

The truth is, even though much of our lives can be seen, much more cannot. Oh, we can show a lot of the outward things—what we're making for dinner, the victories our children had in homeschooling, or even confess how we messed up terribly by losing our patience. But we cannot bare it all. We cannot share everything online. People get only a picture of us. It's simply not possible, not wise, to share it all. Sometimes, we may find ourselves bleeding online, or perhaps the stories we're carrying simply aren't ours to share.

No matter how much is shown, there are aspects of our lives that remain unseen. And there are seasons that we walk through where we feel very much unnoticed, unseen, unfollowed. We may feel like we are failures, like we're stuck, or that we're in a season of sacrifice. We may be wading through pain; have so many responsibilities that we finally say "No

more"; feel more limitations; feel called to lay things down, close doors, and start over. It can be frustrating, isolating, discouraging. Shame may take a part, lies may seep in, and fears may start to whisper.

These are not moments of failure, or setbacks, or seasons that feel like we are simply in survival mode. These are not times to wish away. These are holy moments. Set-apart seasons. God is setting you apart to minister to your heart. He is calling you to come away and be with him. To hear his voice. To be ministered to by his Spirit. To learn to know his voice. To cultivate your soul. To prepare you for the next season ahead, the next mission. He is wanting to meet with you. He is after your heart. For your holiness.

We are not forgotten about, but rather, most *sought after*. Monks will spend hours a day, getting away by themselves, praying and being silent before God. But we mothers don't have time to get away for hours. We are given the privilege of taking care of our kids, and constantly having to lay down our own desires to serve them. From the moment we conceive, or conceive the idea of adopting, we are not our own. Our bodies are theirs. We spend our time thinking and praying for our kids, being up throughout the night nursing, facing early mornings, cooking three meals a day (I've never loved leftovers so much in all my life!), changing diaper after diaper, healing boo-boos, trying to figure out math problems (why is kindergarten math causing my brain to hurt?!), breaking up fights, consoling emotional hurts, leading their little hearts to truth. Our time is simply not our own. While we moms do our best to still get together with our girlfriends, and fill up our souls, and follow dreams, and do what sets our hearts on fire, our lives have changed.

Being a mom isn't the first area in which I've felt unseen, though. Maybe you can relate? I felt unseen when the boy I liked didn't even notice me, when I wasn't included in the friend-group I longed to be a part of, when my limitations looked different from the limitations of those around me. I've felt unseen because my personality is gentle and quiet. I've felt unseen in rooms where no one knows who I am, but everyone knows the person I came with. I've felt unseen in the middle of the night when I'm up alone with a crying baby. I've felt unseen in my hurts and my pain and my season.

But even though I've *felt* unseen, I have always *been* seen. He sees me. He sees you. You never go unnoticed and are never forgotten about. He wants us to put away all the noise and to enter into his presence. To show ourselves to the One who knows every in and out of our very being. He wants us to find joy and contentment in the quiet, in the unseen, so that we can let his presence satisfy our deepest needs. To stop performing, to stop pretending, to stop numbing out. To rest with him, to know deep in our bones that we are not what we do, or what we bring, but we are simply the beloved of God. Being brought close in love so that we can be made more like him.

I have realized that what helps me to hear his voice is to get out for a walk every day. By myself. This in itself is a luxury with little ones at home, but Jeff knows how important it is to me. And when Kannon sees me getting ready to go, he'll ask, "Mom, are you going to talk to Jesus?" I do the same loop, and I always end up pouring out my heart to God. Usually my time on my walk is spent taking what I read that morning, what I'm processing, what I'm struggling through, and working it out with him. "Why do I feel this way? When this happened, it did actually really hurt me. Oh, I see where I was wrong, and I need to ask for forgiveness there." It's a lot of confessing. A lot of God's giving me his eyes to see situations as he does. A lot of his putting others on my heart to pray for them.

God is so patient with us. He doesn't force us to have heart-to-heart moments with him all the time. I think sometimes he knows we simply need a nap, or a good book to laugh with, or a favorite Netflix show to enter into another story. But he's always there, with us, in the pain and the dark and the heavy. In the mundane and the ordinary and the boring. When we cry out to him, he will always hold us, and he will lead us to do the next good thing. He gives us all we need to take the next step, to walk through the next day, to face the hard thing. But we have to go to him, get away with him, pour out our hearts to him in order to find that peace, that resolve, that strength to carry on. An Instagram comment will not fill our souls in the way a verse, his presence, or a friend coming over to pray with us does. A DM will not bring healing the same way as baring your soul in a text conversation with a loved one and having them encourage and pray over you.

This past year, I've fallen pretty silent on social media. I have felt as though the Lord has been looping his arm in mine (often on our walks) and bringing me beside the river, under a shaded tree, to a secret place. He's beckoned me to be more unseen, in the shadows, to meet with him, and to be quiet. To be in a place in my heart where I run to him at the first sign of stress or despair. Where I run to him to find hope and wisdom and comfort. I feel him say, "Let *me* satisfy your weary soul, Alyssa. Let *me* be your wonderful counselor. Let *me* be the One whom you sit with and pour your heart out to. Let *me* hold you, comfort you."

There is not one moment that occurs when you are not seen, friend. His eye is on the sparrow. His eye is on you. And he is delighting in you, and longing for you to enter in. Be quiet. Ask. Listen. Worship. Find deep satisfaction in simply being his.

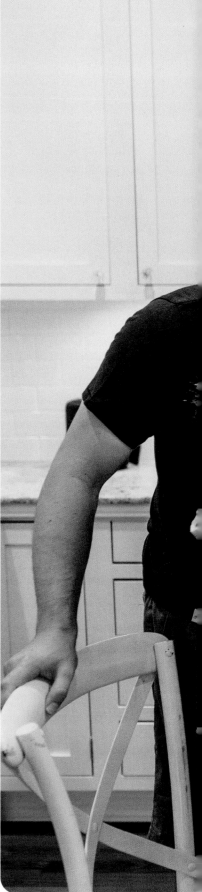

Chapter 3

HIS LOVE

Satisfy us in the morning with your steadfast love,

that we may rejoice and be glad all our days.

PSALM 90:14

’ve heard that every woman should have a special place in her home that is just for her. A special place she can retreat to, where she can get refreshed and cozy up. And if not a spot, then a basket that has all of her special things to fill her up—a good book, a craft, a blanket, a candle, and dark chocolate (can I get an amen?).

I didn't feel like I had that space in our home, so I started to dream of a big chaise lounge in our bedroom where I could read my Bible, write, and snuggle with my kids. At the time, however, finances were tight, so I knew that this would have to be a gift from the Lord—I couldn't just go out and purchase one.

I began to pray and ask Jesus for this desire of my heart. While I don't believe God will give us *all* the things we want, I do believe that he loves to give his children sweet gifts. I decided not to tell Jeff, but to just be faithful to pray about it and see what would happen. This was an opportunity to trust God.

A couple of months passed and nothing.

"Okay, Jesus. I'll keep asking and waiting."

Then one day I saw this beautiful chair on someone's Instastories. I DM'ed her and she pointed me in the right direction. So I checked it out, but the price was a little more than what we could afford.

Now this thing I had been praying for became much more than just a thing. More and more I dreamed of a spot I could call my own; I started to even feel desperate for it. I knew it was a good desire, but somehow it had become something I had to have to be fulfilled as a person. As if by having this chair, all my needs would be met. It's funny the things we'll start to believe that simply are not true. But as most things are, it really was a faith journey for me.

Did I believe that God was good even when I didn't get what I want? Did I believe that he loved me and was for me? Did I believe that my husband loved me and was for me? Did I believe that I had everything I needed in Jesus? Could I hold two truths to be true at the same time—that he loved me and heard my prayers even when they were not answered, or at least not answered on my timetable? Once again, I surrendered this dream to God. I knew I couldn't make it happen.

I decided to go on craigslist early one morning, and there on my phone popped up: "Tommy Bahama White Slipcovered Chaise Lounge." Posted thirty minutes ago.

It was just as I had dreamed. Big, comfy, white slipcover with rolled arms. All my cozy cottage dreams coming true. YES!

Jeff gave the thumbs-up, and I called the lady and told her I would buy it, and when I asked if I could come by in an hour to pick it up, she said, "Well, sure, come by. But we live near Hana, in the jungle; like, there's a waterfall in my backyard. When you get about ten minutes from our home, the road will end and you'll need a 4x4 to continue to the dirt path." Well, that wasn't going to work, so we agreed to pay extra for them to drop it off. She then mentioned that it was a bit musty-smelling. My mom is the queen of cleaning and getting out stains and smells. And it was slipcovered, right? We could just wash it, I told myself.

A few days later, she and her husband dropped off the chair. It was dark when Jeff and I helped unload it from their 4x4 and put it in our bedroom. I noticed a smell at first, but it wasn't terrible, and I knew I could wash it and I even had an upholstery cleaner. We talked and they were so nice, and the slipcover really was well made. I noticed some red dirt stains on the back, but no worries, I had OxiClean.

I retreated to the bedroom to start cleaning it, I was so excited, but a little apprehensive of the smell. I started to take the slipcover off, and noticed a few bugs on the back—cockroaches, spiders, ants. "It's okay," I thought. "It did come from Hana."

I started to get a little nauseated seeing the crawling critters. I quickly killed some and ripped the slipcover off to get it into the washing machine as soon as possible, thinking that would take care of a large part of the problem.

However, even with the slipcover in the wash, the smell was still just as strong. I pulled out my upholstery cleaner and went to work. Vacuumed, cleaned. But the smell wasn't disappearing at all. And then I flipped the chair over to look at the bottom, and, sure enough, there were termite droppings.

You know the feeling when you've been hoping for something, and then, when you finally get it, you realize it's all wrong? You know it wasn't a good use of your money. You made a mistake. That stomach-dropping, heart-pounding, sweaty-palms feeling? Yeah, this was that.

Termites. They're my number one enemy on this little island. So common, and yet the worst houseguest. We've had to throw pieces of furniture away in the past that had termites. This chair wasn't worth enough to justify paying someone to treat it.

That night Jeff woke up in the middle of the night with a huge allergy attack. It was no coincidence. My sweet husband is totally sensitive to smells, and this musty chair was beyond what we could handle.

I called my mom the next morning asking if she could come over and work her magic, and an hour later she arrived with her vinegar spray bottle in hand. She smelled the cushion, and I saw the look of "This is beyond my help." I knew it. This chair was not savable.

Heartbroken, I retreated to our backyard and sat in a rocking chair with our baby Lucy as big tears slid down my face. I had prayed and asked God for the desire of my heart. I had waited. I thought this was the answer to my prayer. I thought Jesus was showing me extra love. I had tried to find a good deal, but we could have used this money on so many other things. I had tried to be detailed and ask all the right questions, and it still wasn't enough.

This had been an act of faith, of hope, of trusting the Lord and believing in his love for me. It was trusting my husband and trying to do good for our family, and then feeling like a huge failure. It was a matter of the heart, and it seemed so big to me.

Jeff came looking for me and found me rocking Lucy, now ugly-crying. He sat in the hammock and I told him all that was on my heart.

"You know, let's just throw the chair away. I can take it to the dump tomorrow. We tried, and it just didn't pan out. Let's figure out another way to get you a chair. We have the savings."

I stopped. "Really?" I whispered.

"Really. You tried so hard, babe. Sometimes things just happen this way. It's not your fault."

I had been overcome with shame and doubt, but the Lord showed me his love through Jeff's grace that day. He patiently listened to my heart and my doubts, and then helped me take that gross piece of furniture to the dump.

Ultimately the Lord did answer my prayers. Yes, he did gift me with the chair of my dreams—I'm sitting on it now as I write this, and yes, it's my favorite spot in our home. But much more so, he answered my deep need of some extra love. I felt loved by the arms of love wrapped around me when I lost it. Of the grace I experienced when I felt like a failure.

Sometimes, it can be easy for me to doubt God's love for me. Sometimes, I don't think he likes me. He doesn't enjoy me much. I wear him out. He's tired of my mistakes and weaknesses. He doesn't like how I handled a situation. He can't believe I'm at this same weak spot, again.

It's easy to believe these things because that's how my heart responds sometimes to others. I'm tired. I don't want to get another snack for my three-year-old. I don't want to fold one more basket of laundry. I don't want to be listening to my husband's new business idea that often makes me feel like I'm out of my comfort zone. I'm annoyed. I'm surprised that *they* haven't overcome that weakness yet. I'm shocked that *I* haven't overcome that weakness yet. I'm worn out over my own sins and mistakes.

Oh, but what love the Father has for us! Grace upon grace. What complete adoration and delight he has for you and me! We are his children, and he takes great joy in us. He loves spending time with us, helping us process our emotions, helping us problem-solve, leading us to truth and wisdom. He loves hearing our hearts confess, and getting to show us grace, again. Because his love never runs dry. It is constant.

Lately I catch myself watching my baby, Lucy, with such delight. I love watching her walk around the room, her cheeks jiggling with every step, bending over, then peering over tables, giggling at our dog, going in for kisses and hugs from her older brother and sister. I love watching her put items where they should go, laughing at the newest discovery, smiling when she's conquered a problem. I think she's the cutest, most adorable person, and I'm completely over the moon for her. Then I stop because I feel as though the Lord is whispering to my heart, "Yes, Alyssa, and I feel the same about you. I love watching you be you. I love watching you discover and grow and learn. I love seeing you do it messily and poorly, but still doing it because you know it's the right thing or the good thing. I love

seeing you seek me; I love seeing you serve your family; I love seeing you teach your kids and laugh with them and read them books and blow bubbles with them. I love watching you kiss your husband and sing an (off-key) hymn to me. I love you being you, not because of anything you do, but because you are mine. I love seeing you bloom into your true self."

Friend, he loves you too. He is completely wild about you. He doesn't love you when you're good or performing at optimal level or when you can check everything off your to-do list. He just loves you because he loves you and he takes great delight in you. He loves you the same when you're the best mom, wife, friend, and aunt as he loves you when you're struggling and weak and losing your patience and have locked yourself in the closet for a little cry session. Nothing, not what you do or don't do, will change his love for you!

I wonder how differently we'd live if we were constantly aware of the Lord's attention on us, and the love that he has for us? If we just sat with that truth for a bit. Let it resonate, and seep into our bones.

God loves me.

God delights in me.

God adores me.

God loves spending time with me.

God loves hearing my thoughts and heart and questions.

God never grows weary or annoyed by me. I'm never too much for him.

I am constantly telling the kids that the only way we can love one another is out of the love that the Father has for us. We cannot do it on our own. And I've seen firsthand as a mom how I can pour out sacrificial love on my family only if I am abiding in the love of the Father. I sometimes feel worn-out and empty. But his love constantly pours into me, so I can pour that love out onto others.

Our Savior is the Lover of our souls and is faithful to pour his love into our hearts, every day, in every moment we turn to him. He wants to show us his love. And when we are filled up, we can then go about our day, loving our people well—not out of an empty cistern, but out of a full one. Ready to listen. Ready to give. Ready to serve. Ready to encourage.

A week later, as I sat recounting the chair story to my friend Sarah over smoothies, she said, "Alyssa, I had a vision today at church. The Lord showed me a vase of flowers, that were in water, well nourished and taken care of. And yet one of the stems had fallen to the ground, needing extra love and sunshine. I felt like someone today was needing a little extra love from Jesus even though they were well taken care of. It was you! And look how he showed you some extra love!"

Tears formed in my eyes. I felt so seen and loved by Jesus in that moment. It was true. I was well watered. I knew God's love for me. I knew how he was with me and was taking care of me through my season of life—all the everyday, hard, good, and trying moments. But I had found myself in a spot needing some extra love. I needed some extra care, extra comfort, extra encouragement.

I didn't *need* that chair. Nor did I deserve to get the one of my dreams. But God, in his abundant grace, gave it to me, in an unlikely way. Grace upon grace. The story could have ended with our taking that chair to the dump, and my finding contentment in the furniture we already had. But instead, God showered me with love from my people and gave me the chair of my dreams. It felt extremely extravagant. Every time I sit in it, I am reminded of how dearly the Lord loves me and how extravagant his love is for me.

And for you, friend.

His love is better than life. We don't have to do anything to earn it; we simply can grab a pink floatie and slowly drift on down his river of love. Resting. Enjoying. Soaking it in. Letting his love move in and through us to accomplish his two greatest commands—to love him with all our heart, and to love others as ourselves.

Chapter 4

GRIEFS HEALED

Even though I walk through the valley of the shadow of death,

I will fear no evil,

for you are with me;

your rod and your staff,

they comfort me.

PSALM 23:4

As I lay on the table, draped in paper for the ultrasound, I couldn't wait to hear her little heartbeat. Our two kids were so excited to gain another brother or sister, and I spent every spare moment dreaming of what three would be like, coming up with different names and imagining my stomach growing with life. I held my breath as the doctor searched for the heartbeat and waited anxiously to see the small life on the screen. The doctor became unusually quiet, and then simply said, "Well, maybe it's earlier than we thought. I don't see a heartbeat yet, but it could be too soon to tell. Why don't you get some bloodwork done to make sure your hormones are increasing, and then come back next week and we'll try again."

My heart sank as tears welled up in my eyes. I left the building feeling like I was having an out-of-body experience. I went through the routine of getting my blood drawn; there were so many vials. But all I could think was, "Wait to cry, Alyssa. Be strong. Wait until you can be safe in your car."

I called Jeff as soon as I could, bawling. We still had hope. Maybe it was too soon? I spent the rest of the day in bed, trying to release my worry to the Lord. Then the next day, I knew. My morning sickness was suddenly gone. Panic set in.

Then it came. The twisting, horrific pain and so much blood. I lay sick in that bed for two weeks. I was so weak that every time I stood up, I felt like I was going to faint. I had to stay close to the bathroom, because in an instant I would feel the blood rush through me. Days went by. It felt like I was living a never-ending day from hell. When she finally passed, my heart ached so deeply, I couldn't make myself leave my bedroom. My mom came and just lay with me in bed. Friends dropped off meals and cards and flowers. My friend Nicole hugged me and cried with me. Jeff was grieving himself, in his own way, while working and taking care of our two older kids. Kinsley would pop in to bring me water, Kannon to give me a kiss. Grief had never felt so close, so horrifying, so suffocating.

I doubted God. I couldn't understand why. I doubted his goodness. I pondered evil and this world and the enemy. I asked Jeff so many questions. I googled sermons and sat with my Bible open. I listened to worship songs, weeping. I binge-watched Hallmark shows.

Eventually, I made it out of my bedroom to the living room. Eventually, my life went on as I grew stronger, in heart and body. Jeff flew me to Sonoma for my birthday a month later, which I thought would be the answer to my healing, only to discover that my healing journey was just beginning. Grief takes time. It's like a person you have no choice but to welcome into your life and become friends with. You can't just run away from it. You can't think that it'll be gone in three easy steps, or after so much time, whatever that timeline is in your head. It'll make unwanted visits when you least expect it.

But eventually, your grief will do a good work in you. Eventually, when it's placed in the nail-scarred hands of Jesus, it will bring redemption. It will bring holiness, depth of

comfort, intimacy with the Savior, and the capacity to empathize with others' pain; it will usher you into a place of true surrender and of being able to trust the God of mystery in a deeper way than you ever did before.

My friend Bianca suggested keeping a tangible thing to remember our little girl, so every time I looked at it, I would think of her. The thing is, no mother forgets her babies. They are forever in our hearts. But when friends or family members talk about our lost ones, it brings such a comfort knowing that they remember too. And seeing something tangible, as if our sweet little baby is with us still, or, rather, that God is whispering to our hearts that our babies are with him, being held in his arms, brings a deep sense of comfort.

I started to pray about what that tangible object could be, when one day I drove home and there on my doorstep was a gardenia plant. Bianca left a note saying, "For every time a gardenia blooms, we will remember her." I cried. God has given me the sweetest friends. Gardenias are my favorite plant with the sweetest fragrance, which I will now always connect with the memory of our sweet girl.

I took that plant to our backyard and would sit next to it in the mornings as I had my quiet time. I would take my lunch outside and eat beside it. I would read picture books to the kids right next to it. I was starting to feel my heart slowly mending, but then thoughts began to flicker through my mind: "I'm not able. I'm not capable. I can't do it.

"All of it. Any of it.

"I couldn't carry my baby to full term.

"I couldn't keep up with the demands of my day. I couldn't be the friend I needed to be, or serve the Lord like I thought he was asking of me."

I told myself it wasn't true, and moved on.

Then those thoughts came back and made their home in my mind and heart. I mentioned them to my husband, my mom, and one of my mentors at different times, and they all said, "Alyssa, you know that's not true, right? You know that's not how it works. You can't let yourself believe that." And I would quietly nod and agree. I knew the thoughts were wrong. And yet, I couldn't let them go.

I couldn't shake the idea that somehow it was my fault. I went through all the thoughts that a mom has when she loses her baby. All the things I did that could have caused it. But at the end of the day, what I really believed was that regardless of what had caused it, *I* wasn't able to carry her. *I* wasn't enough. *I* wasn't able. *I* didn't have what it took to have a healthy baby, not anymore anyway.

That thought morphed and grew and took precedence in my life. It greeted me and paralyzed me throughout the week: "I can't do it. I don't have what it takes. I'm incapable. Unable." And the tricky thing about the lies was that they held some truth. Slightly. Yes, it was and is true that I am weak. I'm human. I'm not God. I have limitations. And God knows my frame. He has made me to need him. He constantly is telling us in Scripture to rest in him, to abide in him; that we can't do anything apart from him. That in our weakness, he is powerful.

Those lies totally diminished who God is. He also says that we can do all things in and through him. That he has given us his Spirit, that when we abide in him, he carries us. That we are more than conquerors through Christ who strengthens us.

The lies wreaked havoc on my life. I woke up in the morning and felt paralyzed. Like I couldn't get through the day. I didn't have what it took to be pregnant again. To care for two toddlers and their hearts' needs. I didn't have what it took to keep a home, or be a good friend, or a loyal daughter. And I certainly didn't have what it took to keep up with my energetic, on-the-go, visionary husband. I crumbled when he talked about traveling and setting out on new adventures and starting new businesses. It all seemed too much. I simply was not created to do all of that.

Although I had healed from my grief of losing our baby, I still carried trauma. That happens with any traumatic event in life. Trauma looks different for every person and in different seasons. Breaking up with a boyfriend, a divorce, a betrayal, an abuse, a sickness, or a rejection; one moment gone sour can turn life upside down.

And when that trauma was triggered, I felt broken. Once again. Weak and messy and incredibly vulnerable. God revealed my trauma, but it seemed so deep and permanent, I didn't know where to start to begin healing all over again. One night, as I lay in my bed with tears streaming down my face, hugging my body pillow, I felt the Lord's silence. He didn't speak to my heart right then.

But as the days progressed, I realized God was meeting me right where I was. That's the beauty of him. He doesn't expect us to do it. *He* does it. *He* is the Healer. *He* is the Rescuer. We simply have to cry out to him. Turn to him; be open to him. Ask for help. Pour out our hearts of doubt and hurt and confusion. And he comes. Always. In his own unique way, for our own unique soul. He knows what we need, when we need it. He knew the exact time to reveal my brokenness and trauma. He spoke to me through a forgotten journal, a new verse, a song that comforted me in that season of grief.

One night our small group went around and told each other what God had spoken over us as our identity. As I shared how I was fighting to believe God's truths about me and put off the lies I believed about myself, my friend Jess looked me in the eyes and read over

a list of identities God had given her about me. One of them was that I was not strong by myself, but I was *empowered by the Spirit*, and that made me strong.

So I began another healing journey. Healing journeys always begin with our brokenness. Our humility and surrender. No healing journey is easy. It doesn't happen overnight and it takes hard work. To surrender those lies daily, sometimes moment by moment, and to take on God's truth. To ask for his Spirit's help. To open our eyes to see his truth and reality and to be full of his hope.

We are hand in hand with Jesus. Weak, but empowered. Broken, yet hope-filled. Messy, but grace-sustained.

Shortly after that small group meeting, I felt a longing to create and make something beautiful. I asked Carla, an amazing painter in our community, if she would teach me how to paint our favorite beach. After she gave me a lesson, I felt alive and started thinking about painting every day. As I drove I would notice different colors I had never seen before, or wonder how I would paint the light in a certain scene. I made a little spot in our house to set up an easel and bought paint and brushes and painted every opportunity I had. Creating something beautiful healed parts of my soul. When I felt like I had failed to create life, creating art brought healing.

One day, I set a little gardenia plant on my patio table to paint. I needed to paint, to focus on something beautiful. Sitting there, giving thanks for God's gift to us, remembering how he never left my side as I grieved, and still grieve now, for our loss. I had no idea how to paint white flowers (they're much trickier than you would think!), but as I sat there listening to worship music, my hair in a braid, wearing my apron with lemons on it and focusing on this flower, something in me started to stir. Hope. Hope had finally come. It had taken much longer than I had anticipated, but like a little bud on the plant, hope was budding in my heart once again. I could see redemption being played out. I could trust my Savior's care for me, our family, and for our baby now in heaven. I still grieved, but I could give thanks for how God held me through it all, and was still holding her.

It's definitely not the greatest painting I've done, but painting the gardenia healed a deep part of my soul. It's hanging in our living room, and every time I think I should switch it out for something different, I can't. Because it's part of me, part of us. Because it was something I made *for* her.

Gardenias will forever remind me of our little girl, Ellie Grace. Every morning on my walk I'm greeted by multiple gardenia trees, and I always stop to smell their sweet fragrance. Ellie, you are such a sweet aroma to us; even in your death, you have brought us life.

Chapter 5

SLOW MIRACLES

Every good gift and every perfect gift is from above, coming down from the Father of lights with whom there is no variation or shadow due to change.

JAMES 1:17

It had been a *week*. My mom took the older kids for a couple of hours in the morning so I could get some things done around the house and have some quiet. When they came home at noon, they had huge smiles on their faces, each having picked out a bouquet of flowers that they thought I would like best. It touched my heart in so many ways and humbled me, since I sure didn't feel like I deserved flowers after how I had reacted to the chaos of the week. Those bouquets represented so much grace.

I laid out the bouquet that Kannon had gotten me and started to cut the stems and place them in my cute farmhouse pitcher. These cheerful pink gerbera daisies smiled up at me, and just as I was going to throw away the wrapping that they came in, I saw something sparkling next to the little bag of flower food. It was a ring—a huge platinum, diamond, and sapphire ring! I immediately looked at my finger, wondering if my wedding ring had fallen off, but nope, it was still there. Then I thought the found ring had to be fake, since it was so big and shiny. But when I picked it up it was heavy, and I knew it was too beautiful to be fake.

When I showed it to my mom, she picked it up, examined it. We looked at each other with our mouths open in shock. "We gotta call the store where we bought the flowers," my mom said. Sure enough, the guy on the other line said a lady had reported losing her diamond ring somewhere in the store two days ago. He wasn't sure what to do next, though, so my mom called again, this time asking for the manager. "Oh, sure, bring it in and drop it off. We'll figure it out when we get a chance." Uh, yeah right. This is someone's wedding ring. We're not just going to drop it off.

That night when my parents were headed home, they stopped by the store. When my mom heard that the missing ring's description was an exact match to the one she held in her hand, she asked for the phone number to call the owner.

She called and told the lady the tale, who immediately started crying. "I have to meet you. I can't believe it. I was praying that God would let it show up. It's my engagement ring. My boyfriend sold his car to buy it for me—a one-and-a-half-carat Vera Wang with sapphires. I was worried sick. I can't believe you found it!"

What were the odds that she would even know she lost her ring at the store? It could have been in so many places, but it happened to be in one bouquet of flowers that my son happened to pick up. He even had picked it out, put it back, and then picked it out again. It could have been thrown away, or someone might have found it but kept the ring. And then the fact that I actually saw the ring—it was hidden in there. I could have easily been so distracted talking to my mom or prepping dinner that I might have missed it and just thrown it away with the paper.

Truly, I got to witness a miracle. I got to be a part of God's work and see a picture of how big and all-knowing he is. How he answers prayers. And it was such a delight and joy and uplift to my harried week!

Sometimes in our lives, if we open our hearts and eyes to see, we will get to witness miracles. Big and extravagant and unreal miracles that leave us in awe. Just this year I've seen two miracles: my dad's cancer being wiped away when we thought we were going to lose him; and a friend conceiving after fourteen years of infertility! I just want to weep every time I think about those miracles. But more often than not, the miracles we witness are slow. They take time—weeks, months, years. They usually involve a lot of pain, surrender, hours of prayer, seeking counsel, laying down our pride and putting on humility. These slow miracles involve Jesus' carrying us through the pain and unknown. Waiting and patience and day-in, day-out faith are required. Over and over again offering the pain, the anguish, the desire, the plea to the Lord and waiting on him to act.

Working through issues in your marriage. Two becoming one, learning to truly open up and trust each other and learn how to be completely vulnerable and to be a safe place for the other, to call each other out and to become your glorified selves.

Helping your child grow, learning to listen to God's voice, seeing them love their siblings and become empathetic.

Having a child, family member, or friend give their life to Jesus; to surrender, to call out to him, to lay down their life and be saved.

Working hard, faithfully saving and putting away and knocking out that debt one payment at a time.

Having a dream that is beyond your capability or provision and, one step at a time, making progress toward it. One step in front of the other, often all the ground gained being the Lord's moving and directing and opening doors, and our simply being available and willing in all the small ways.

Finding restoration between friends or family members. Constantly choosing to be *for* them, to humble ourselves and ask for forgiveness, to be honest about hurt, to choose to love them and pray for them, even if we have to agree to disagree; to put boundaries in place, to constantly go back to those boundaries to evaluate how the restoration is going.

Waiting on a desire that's unfulfilled. A spouse. A child. A home. A job. A dream. Praying. Surrendering. Making a step forward, saying yes to something, or hearing the Lord's voice telling you to wait and see. Sometimes having everything feel so dark, uncertain; feeling as though you're going to suffocate if you have to wait. One. More. Minute.

We don't usually notice slow miracles. We want sudden change, prayers answered within a day; we want to know what the plan is, avoid the pain, be in control, enjoy the fruit. But just because we don't see the fruit right away, have the victory, know the outcome, have full restoration, or see the longing fulfilled doesn't mean there's no progress. Doesn't mean God isn't *actively* at work on achieving a miracle at that very moment.

There is so much we don't see. So much going on behind the scenes. And God promises to use it all for our good. So our waiting is not in vain. Our pain is not in vain. As Job says, "I know that you can do all things, and that no purpose of yours can be thwarted" (Job 42:2). Our groaning, crying out, pleading, seeking, taking steps toward peace and restoration, humbling ourselves, searching our hearts—it's all being used to conform us to be more and more like Jesus. To become who we really are. And to draw us to himself. To enter into the inner courts to get to know our Savior more. The Savior who is fully acquainted with our griefs. Who bears our pain. Who sits and cries with us. Who holds us in his arms, and offers us so much hope. The One who has the power to transform lives, to reveal, to shine light on darkness, to bring the kingdom to earth. He is King and he is on his throne, and even if it doesn't feel like it, he is at work right now, in your situation. He is for you.

So we continue to cry out to God, to ask him for the miracles. For the restoration and the gift and the wisdom. And we put on our faith glasses to see what he sees. To look for all the ways he answers our prayers—all the little ways. And we take note of them. Write them down. Cherish his answers in our hearts. Remember, so we can walk forward in faith.

Perhaps this life is made up of small miracles. Of looking for all the little ways the Lord loves us and is at work. Of how he is holding all things in his hands, and holds all things together.

I'm learning to look at liturgy this way. I think little habits we do free us to be the people we long to be. To pursue those habits that form us to become our glorified selves. We can't just wait until we *feel* like doing something, because often the very things that are good for us are not necessarily what we feel like doing. But the more we do them, choosing to do the hard things, little by little, one, five, ten minutes at a time, is what will transform our souls. And that's the miracle.

But it takes intentionality. Getting away and asking ourselves who we want to become, who we want our families to become, and then backtracking and choosing one little step that is doable, to implement. One little step at a time. If you want to be a woman who loves Jesus and trusts him, then you need to spend time with him. Open his Word and read, one verse at a time. One prayer at a time. If you want to be a mom who is present with her kids, then you may need to put your phone in the cabinet for an hour from 3 to 4 p.m. each day. If you want to have intentional time together as a family, you might spend snack time each afternoon reading a story with your kids. If you want to be a family who uplifts one another and cheers one another on, you might go around the dinner table one night a week and each of you say one thing you love about a certain family member. If you want to be a runner, you don't sign up for a marathon tomorrow, but you do need to put some running shoes on and get outside and start running. Doesn't have to be every day. Doesn't have to be five miles at a time. It could be ten minutes twice a week, but that makes you a runner. You don't have to aim for perfection, or 100 percent even. We're not looking for A+'s. We're simply learning to be the people we want to be—living in the 80 percent rule. Rhythms over goals. Intentionality over reacting. Being present over distraction. Grace over legalism.

The wedding ring miracle was a once-in-a-lifetime experience. We will get to witness some of those, but most of our lives are made up of the small, everyday miracles. Answered prayers, yes, but also the miracle of a tomato that grows in our garden, the miracle of our kids laughing together, of a child learning a new concept, of connecting with our husbands; the miracle of feeling known through a conversation with a friend, of the comfort of a hug, the encouragement of a handwritten note, air-conditioning! If we choose to see life through the lens of faith and thankfulness, we will see the everyday miracles.

One day our faith will be turned into sight. One day our pain will be completely gone. But while we wait, we can have true, sure hope because God is trustworthy and he cares for us. He gives us every good gift, and he is a God who works miracles. That's what he does. He's in the business of miracles. It's a funny thing to be in between. To believe in the God of miracles and yet wait on him for ours. To believe he can work and answer our prayers and yet to be content when perhaps his answer is different from what we thought it would be. To wait with hope and yet find our true satisfaction while we wait.

But mark this: Just because we may not see our miracle doesn't mean there is no miracle. Perhaps our miracle looks a lot different from what we expected. Or perhaps the miracle isn't in the gift, but rather in the process of who we are becoming while we wait on him. The process of finding our satisfaction in him as our greatest longing is fulfilled.

God gives such good gifts, but the sweetest thing of all is that *we get God*. He is our gift. And he will be with us in every longing, during the long wait, and after. He is with us always. He is with us as we kneel on the floor and ask him, again. As we walk around our neighborhood, asking, again. As we crawl into our closet with tears in our eyes crying out to him and asking, again. He will be with us as we enter the new season, the new thing he has miraculously done, but we find our steps to be shaky, and the outcome not quite what we imagined. As we encounter hard days, still; longings unfulfilled, still. Ideals not quite so ideal. Even in the yeses we still need God, and the good news is that he always gives all of himself. He is the same God in the waiting as in the receiving.

Chapter 6

WEARY HEARTS REJOICE

I'll refresh tired bodies;

I'll restore tired souls.

I love music. My mom was always singing and playing the piano at home. She sang in the church choir and on the worship team. When I was five, I used to put on a show for my parents every night after dinner, and I often charged them ten cents to watch! When my grandparents would visit, Grandma Gigi would let me wear one of her fancy fur coats for my performance. I grew up in choir and doing musical productions. Once I was a camel's behind (I was destined for greatness at an early age). I loved being part of our youth group's worship team and spent countless nights staying up late practicing songs with my friends or staying late at church preparing for Sunday's service. And later, music played an important role in our family life. Jeff and I loved sharing mixed CDs (remember those?), worship songs, musicals, concerts, and dance parties with our kids.

I think God created music because he knew that it would bring joy to our hearts as it does to his. When I think of some of the most fun moments of my life, where I've felt free and have been doubled over with joy and laughter and merriment, those moments have involved music. Dancing to "Gangnam Style" at our wedding, doing the "Cupid Shuffle" at other weddings, singing at the top of my lungs with girlfriends as we drove down the highway with the top down, dancing with the kids in the kitchen after dinner to "Can't Stop the Feeling." And when I have felt most comforted and able to express my deep emotions, it's also been with music. Weeping during a worship song, on my knees, plucking away at the piano keys or guitar strings as I clumsily learn a new song. When I could not express my pain, when I could not muster hope, when I could not come up with the right words to give someone, music has stepped in.

But as we walked through a tough year, music took a backseat. Praise was hard to come by. It seemed like I mostly just pleaded to God. I found myself longing to have a good laugh, but coming up dry. Every time I sang at church, I would end up just weeping through the playlist. I was so tired. We had bad news after bad news. Once we thought we were finished with a hardship, another sad thing hit or that old one came back in a new form, another layer. I made it through my days, but I simply didn't have much zest for life. I wasn't necessarily just surviving, but I definitely was not thriving. I tried my best to stay healthy and hopeful, but only because God held me the whole way.

I started asking the Lord, "Have I done something wrong? Are you tired of me? Am I just complaining all the time? Is it okay to be sad?" And I was confronted with the question: Will I still hope in the Lord when the trials of life leave me so bone-weary? When the pain continues, when the questions aren't answered, when I'm still longing and waiting? While I'm grieving and distressed, can I still hope in him?

True hope has to be exercised in the unseen. We hope for what we cannot see. It usually involves life's not being what we hoped it would be, not what we expected, and leaving us longing for more. Hope is often paired with pain or grief; otherwise, we wouldn't need it.

My reality was that waves of bad news kept coming like the tide. And in truth, I'm still a bit shaken over the hard conversations that took place, the words that were said, more bad news coming, fear and worry taking root in my heart; however, God was right beside me the entire way. Not one day passed where he was not holding my hand in the fire, his heart hurting with mine. But it didn't stop there.

God was wanting to renew my mind with his Word, to make me strong and steadfast and to engrave true hope into my heart. I languished and doubted and came to him weary and exhausted, but he wanted me to keep having the hard conversations, keep pursuing unity and peace as much as I could, keep praying and pleading and boldly coming before him. Keep hoping. Keep filling my mind with his truth. Instead of telling myself it was so hard over and over and over, he wanted me to renew my thoughts with his truth. Then I started listening to the hymn "'Tis So Sweet to Trust in Jesus." Over and over, the words made their way into my soul. "I'm so glad I learned to trust him" and "I know that he is with me." Eventually, I stopped focusing on all that was so awful and broken, and I started

to ponder what good work he was doing through it. How was he developing my character? How was my hope being strengthened? I was enduring, through him. "I'm so glad I learned to trust him."

When I actually praise Jesus with my lips and sing to him, it does something to me. How many times have I started to sing to him when I didn't necessarily feel like it, and immediately started crying because it touched my soul? To be together with other believers and hear them sing their hearts to Jesus, to sing an anthem of trust and praise to him, how that stirs my faith and opens my eyes and heart to truly see his goodness and greatness. Music brings praise during the hardships of life—and even joy in the midst of the mundane.

Often, it's hard for me to bring up a verse or truth about God when I'm deep in despair, or when the load of my day feels too heavy. But how often do I have a tune, a song, running through my head? Singing stirs my heart when I am out of touch with my feelings, it strengthens my faith and helps me to look up. Jeff and I decided to be intentional in teaching our kids that as well.

Sometimes I find a hymn on YouTube, and we sing it together and worship snuggled up on the couch together. Not everyone sings and it can be awkward at times, and sometimes the kids beg for a different song. But we're staying faithful. One hymn every month or two, until we know all the words. Sometimes I look up the simple and straightforward version; sometimes a worship band has a rendition that I love and use. But we sit there on the couch for those four minutes and worship Jesus. And I feel my hurry and my fears and my frustrations start to melt away, and I rejoice at the truth of those songs, and at Kinsley singing along next to me, and at how anthems of truth are being built into our hearts. Singing as I change diapers and prep dinner and give baths. It's always a bit chaotic and never as dreamy as I picture, but storing those words of truth in our hearts is worth the imperfections. It brings the greatest comfort to my heart to know that one day the kids will pull up these songs they've stored in their hearts as they rock their babies to sleep or run that half marathon or study late into the night.

My hope is that they will turn to these truths when they face adversity. While I hope they won't experience it, the reality is that this life is full of pain. People will hurt us; words will heap shame and guilt and fear over us. We will have bad news; the diagnosis will be worse than what we expected; we will lose loved ones. We may have to make huge sacrifices, let things go, take big risks because we know God is asking us to. We may lose money, relationships, and be forced to have difficult conversations. We'll be asked to make hard decisions, stand up for what we believe is true, step in to protect people, step back to protect our families and boundaries. We may be asked to do something that we have feared all our lives. We will be asked to do the really hard things. We will be brought to the end of ourselves. Grief may intrude into our lives and worry may knock every morning when we wake up. We may feel alone in it all. Friends may dwindle because friendships sometimes are deepened or broken through pain.

God never promised that this life would be easy. He in fact warned us that it would be hard. But he gave us a promise: He will be with us through it all. We are never alone. He goes through the fire with us, friends. And we will not be burned (see Isa. 43:2b). The enemy comes to steal, kill, and destroy, but God allows only what will mature and sanctify us. He allows only what will make us holy. And the God of redemption will redeem all things for his glory. He wins back a situation. He frees from distress. He helps to overcome something detrimental. He restores and repairs and makes it worthwhile.

The pain that you may be facing right now or will face at some future date in your journey, the pain that you walked through last year, will be made worthwhile. He is at work in us, always ministering to our hearts through it all.

While last year was a time of weeping and mourning for us, this year laughter and dancing have come. But even through the hurt, praises were what carried me, without my even realizing it. Worship songs sent to me, others singing alongside me at church, worship music in the background of our days, every day. I felt carried by song last year. And this year, as the cloud has slowly rolled away and the sun has warmed up our days, dancing and laughter are more easily available. Dance parties are more common, and songs sung come from a place of deep knowing—for truly I can sing about how good my God is because he has proved it to me. Joy does come in the morning, and whether we are being carried by the music, held by others' prayers, or able to sing ourselves and shout aloud of God's grace and goodness, praising him is what carries us through the storms of life. It is what makes our lives full of color. Praises proclaim his story of faithfulness.

As the psalmist said,

> Sing praises to the LORD, O you his saints,
>> and give thanks to his holy name.
> For his anger is but for a moment,
>> and his favor is for a lifetime.
> Weeping may tarry for the night,
>> but joy comes with the morning.

(PSALM 30:4–5 ESV)

Part II

Chapter 7

TRAP OF
COMPARISON

Make a careful exploration of who you are and the work
you have been given, and then sink yourself into that.
Don't be impressed with yourself. Don't compare yourself
with others. Each of you must take responsibility for doing
the creative best you can with your own life.

GALATIANS 6:4–5 MSG

When we moved to Maui, finding community, putting in the time to make roots and cultivate strong relationships, took so much longer than I anticipated. It took more risk, vulnerability, and courage too. Honestly, I was really insecure in who I was, what I had to offer, where I fit in, and how life was done here, on top of figuring out how to be a mom, how to be a wife (we were still early into our marriage), and how to take care of our first home. Then I got pregnant again, which always tends to make me feel not myself. I have a love-hate relationship with hormones.

While Laura is now a great friend, comparison took root in my heart when we first met. As I was getting to know her, I admired so many things about her. She is so creative, such a great mom and can accomplish more in an hour than I can on any given day. However, instead of cherishing these things about her, I found myself comparing myself to her every time we chatted and came away feeling convicted. I knew this was prohibiting me from becoming close to someone whom I really wanted to be friends with. Admiration turned into comparison. Inspiration turned into despair. It left me feeling dissatisfied, stressed, ungrateful, confused, and insecure. Truth be told, the comparison was eating away at my soul and feeding my insecurities and fears. It was becoming a huge barrier in my friendship and stealing so much joy and freedom.

Finally, one day I'd had enough. I was done playing this isolating game in my mind. I asked Jesus to forgive me for everything. For not loving my sister, for being ungrateful for all his gifts to me, for letting discontentment rule in my heart. For setting up standards of what I should be doing, of what my life should look like, that were not of the Lord. I confessed how insecure I felt, and asked Jesus to let me see my life and my friend through his eyes. Making the comparisons didn't disappear overnight, but slowly, day by day, every time we connected, I was able to turn more of my comparisons into thanksgiving.

"Lord, thank you for how you wired my friend to be so creative. She is able to accomplish a lot and I so admire her strength and courage. I love the mom she is, the woman she is. Thank you that I can talk with her and learn from her."

Laura truly has been a great friend, and I am ever so grateful for her friendship. But if I had not laid down those insecurities, if I had not confessed my tendency to compare myself to her, I would have missed out on a sweet friendship. Laura encourages me, inspires me, and challenges me. I am truly a better person because she is in my life.

This comparison trap runs deep. It's been going on since the beginning of time. We're not immune to it, no matter how lovely, seemingly perfect, or successful our lives are. We will always have to fight the thoughts that the grass is greener on the other side; the desire to be more like *her*, and the doubt that our lives are playing out the way we hoped.

Why do we compare? What is at the core of it? I believe we fall into the trap when we doubt God's story that he has written for us. Jeremiah 29:11 says, "For I know the plans I have for you, declares the LORD, plans for welfare and not for evil, to give you a future and a hope."

Before we were born, God had all our days written for us (see Ps. 139), and as the author of our lives, he has a good story written for each of us. Yes, as with all good stories, they include tragedy and sorrow and pain. Longings and desires, disappointments and setbacks. Not because God wrote those in, but because we live in a fallen world and are flesh. We will experience pain because we are not home yet. But as our good Father, he redeems all things. He is writing something beautiful. He is writing a story that will bring great glory to himself, that will bring hope to many through *you*. Your story is a *good* one. It includes a future full of hope and goodness.

Each of our stories is unique because of our individual personalities, how we see the world, our passions and giftings. Where we live, whom we live with, the experiences we have. But when we lose sight of that truth, when we take our eyes off his authorship, and we look at our lives and see that they're not exactly playing out as we hoped or as we planned, and we experience pain or struggles, we doubt. We want to take the pen and write a new story, one that is more acceptable to us.

We look around at other women and want little pieces of their stories. We want their successes. Their giftings, their looks, their accomplishments. Their eyelashes, their knowledge, their passion.

And let's be honest. Social media as a whole doesn't make it easy on us. Every time we open our phones and scroll, we are bombarded with images and beauty and stories of other women living their (what seem to be) perfect and pulled-together and amazing lives. We see everyone's fashion attire, homes, mothering, homeschooling, after-school sports, family lives, and careers on display. Even though we get only a glimpse, we can easily feel like we're being bombarded with others' stories that can cause us to feel less than, unable, failing, and missing the mark of being the ideal woman.

But friend, you are not *her*.

You are you.

And this world needs *you*.

Not a you who's more like *her*.

But *you*.

A strong, confident, humble you.

A woman who keeps her eyes on Jesus and knows who she is in him.

A woman who rests in her identity in Christ.

You are God's daughter, and you are loved, cherished, and wonderfully made. You were given gifts and talents to be used for his kingdom. You bring light and beauty to this world in your own unique way.

We have to fight these thoughts of comparison. Those thoughts that seem to taunt us regarding who we *aren't* and who we *should* be. Or who we *wish* we were. Instead, we need to ask God who we *are* in him, to see the good gifts that he has given each one of us, to see the story that he is writing for us, and to step into it. We need to face our realities head-on, link arms with other women to help fight the good fight, and become our best selves. That may mean unfollowing someone, or deleting an app, or turning off our phones for an hour, a day, a season. We have to be vigilant in guarding our thoughts and eyes so that we can have victory in the battle.

How has God created you to bring beauty to this world? Only you can be you. You're the only you in your family, your community, your workspace, your small group, on your college campus. Acts 17:26 (ESV) says, "And he made from one man every nation of mankind to live on all the face of the earth, having determined allotted periods and the boundaries of their dwelling place." He didn't place her there at this time, he placed you. The world and those closest to you need you, not her.

This story that God is writing is like a huge tapestry. A beautiful embroidered treasure filled with bright colors and different stitches. If we are not who he's created us to be, we are taking away from the bigger picture. It's like we're forfeiting our part of the embroidery, which will leave it incomplete, unfinished, and confusing to the beholder. We need every part, every color, every string, every stitch to make up what he has set forth in motion. Don't get stuck in the trap of jealousy and comparison.

It's exhausting to try to be someone we're not. To always be thinking of what we should do. We need to be growing, changing, and continuing to lay down our sins at his feet so that we become the glorified, true, best versions of ourselves. But let's not get that mixed up with becoming someone else. Become your best self, whom God has set forth and spoken over you.

We are God's workmanship. We're his masterpieces. God created each one of us. He had a plan and a purpose for our lives before time even began, and he handcrafted us to be unique and bring beauty to the world, each in our own way. No, we won't all have the perfect fashion sense, the cleanest house, be able to juggle it all, or have a Pinterest-perfect life. We won't all have a platform or be an influencer or run a business or open an Etsy shop. We can't be everything we admire in everyone we know. We can't do foster care and host people all the time and make the most delicious bread and look like an ad for our local gym and homeschool and travel all over the country and lead five Bible studies and restore furniture on the side.

Let's learn from each other. Let's be inspired by one another. And let's fight against comparison. Against the lie that we have to do it all and be good at everything. Against the lie that we're not enough, that what we have is not enough.

You. Are. Enough. Because God is enough in you. More than enough.

This world needs you.

We need the beauty that you bring to this earth in your own original way. Give thanks for the person God created her to be, and then give thanks for the person he has made you to be. And if you aren't sure who that is, ask. Ask him to show you your gifts, the beauty that you bring to the world, the passions set within you. Ask him how to see your life—your personality, energy level, passions, physical blessings, responsibilities, knowledge, creativity—through his eyes. Let yourself bloom and flourish in his love and care for you. Bloom into your best self. Let's be women who are rooted and secure in who we are. And then we can cheer others on to do the same.

breakfast benediction

I'M NOT WHAT I DO.
I'M NOT WHAT I HAVE.
I'M NOT WHAT
PEOPLE SAY ABOUT
ME. I AM THE BE-
LOVED OF GOD. IT'S
WHO I AM.
NO ONE CAN TAKE IT
FROM ME. I DON'T
HAVE TO HURRY. I
DON'T HAVE TO
WORRY. I CAN TRUST
MY FRIEND JESUS
AND SHARE HIS LOVE
WITH THE WORLD.

Chapter 8

FIGHTING FOR FAITH

Fear not, for I am with you;

be not dismayed, for I am your God;

I will strengthen you, I will help you,

I will uphold you with my righteous right hand.

ISAIAH 41:10

We were sitting in our living room, snacks scattered on the coffee table, sharing our hearts and struggles with our mentors, Jeremy and April, who are full of wisdom, grace, and humility. Jeff and I couldn't seem to get past this big topic that we have argued about since before we were married. It finally had come to a point where we were desperate for wisdom and intervention.

As we shared, tears welled up in my eyes. I remember Jeremy looking at me and asking, "What are you scared of?"

As I shared, I could tell that my fears sounded illogical, but in my mind, they were perfectly sane. My hands were trembling. My body started to break out in a sweat. "I'm just a fearful person," I admitted.

Then Jeremy gave words to my struggle, and the Spirit's arms of conviction and comfort wrapped around me in a hug. "It sounds like you've made an agreement with fear." He went on to share how he had made an agreement with a different lie a few years ago, and told me his journey of confessing it to the Lord and turning from those false beliefs he had succumbed to for years. His honesty opened my eyes to see my own agreement and broke my heart. I had been *choosing* to be fearful.

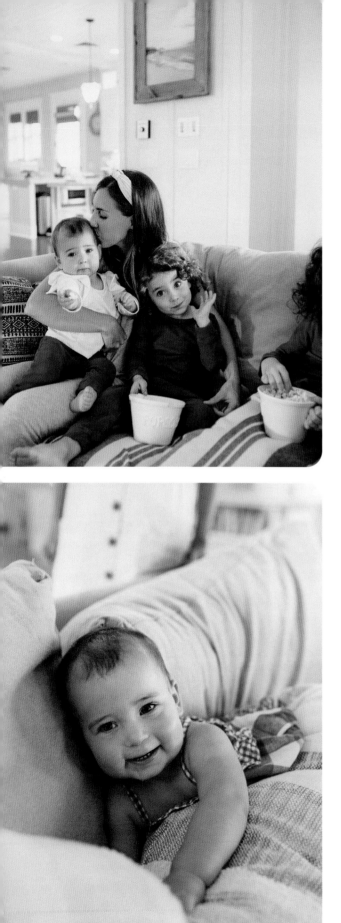

I had made an agreement that was not of the Lord. For years I had been telling myself that I was a fearful person. *I just am.* I knew the Lord didn't want me to fear, that in him fear fled and that this was not what he had planned for me. But how many times had I confessed my fear, and it still came back like an unwelcome houseguest? How many times had I struggled with fear, and instead of rejoicing at my victory over it, it seemed to grow bigger and bigger in my mind until I closed myself off? Off from truth. Off from people speaking truth over me. Off from my husband. No matter what I did, my fear did not leave. I didn't *feel* less frightened. My worry still stuck around. Low-level anxiety was a constant in my life. God had the victory, but this battle was too exhausting and I didn't see fruit quickly enough, so I would admit defeat and stop fighting because that was who I was.

I've always struggled with fear in some way, whether it was the fear of failure, of missing out, of not being enough, or of not having control. And since Jeff and I were engaged, I've struggled with traveling. I love that it's part of our job and calling, and we have made a million memories; however, the unknown, the disruptions to our normal, the long hours and long flights, and having little ones who still require four suitcases each because of diapers and pack-and-plays and strollers is hard for this homebody girl who loves her routine and knowing what to expect in a day. It simply seems completely out of my control, and that feels *scary.* And if we don't all go, then it usually means I'm parenting by myself for an extended period of time. While I love my special time with the kids, I am constantly wondering, "Can I do this? Will we be okay?"

Since I had made an agreement with myself that I was indeed a fearful person, it seemed like I was unable to *not* be fearful. I couldn't fight those overwhelming feelings because I believed that no matter what I did, I would always be that way; I would always struggle. And, honestly, I was tired of fighting. I believed that was who I was, and I didn't believe that God was powerful enough to help me.

Sometimes the fear was so thick I had trouble breathing. My breaths felt shallow; my heart raced; my mind got foggy. Even after Jeremy and April walked us through some counseling and how my fears affected our marriage, my fear did not disappear. It didn't suddenly go away when I confessed it to the Lord. But my thinking was now different. I knew that I could no longer say, "I'm just a fearful person," or "Fear will always have a hold on me." I couldn't use that excuse anymore; I couldn't believe that lie.

Rather, when I felt fearful, I knew that I was trying to tight-fist my life. My hands were closed, trying to hold my life and the unknowns and things I had no control over closely. I had to practice opening my hands, taking deep breaths, and reminding myself that God was Warrior King. Even though I still felt some decisions were too much for me, God gave me the grace to hope, trust, and release.

When traveling for the first time with the three kids, I was a nervous wreck. Then, traveling alone with Lucy as a newborn left me shaking and taking deep breaths every minute. Having my dad receive news that he had bladder cancer, and not being sure if he was going to live, caused my heart to break in two. Having our business collapse, and not knowing if we were going to make ends meet, caused some panic. And having Jeff leave for three weeks on a book tour while I solo-parented three kids under age five was like facing my biggest giant. I would wake up every morning with short breaths, not able to focus on my Bible reading, feeling like my heart would jump out of my chest. I was so fearful during that time as I struggled to entrust my fears to the Lord. Everything I normally got anxious about and worried over kept coming in like the ocean waves, one after another.

But I remembered that I was not defined by my fear. I was the Lord's, and the Lord was on my side. He fights our battles for us, so every morning I would turn on my meditation album that led me through different passages of Scripture and led me through breathing exercises, and there I would confess and admit my fear, and be still before my Father. I would lay my burdens at his feet, yet again, and cry out to him.

Oh, friends, I was fearful and felt like I was crumbling. But the difference was, this time I began to fight and I stayed in the game. I went to my Father again and again and again. At 6 a.m., 10 a.m., noon, 3 p.m., 6 p.m., 9 p.m. I listened to worship music, I thought on Scripture, I wrote a million notes next to many psalms. And it was there, in my hot mess, in my absolutely fear-stricken state, that he met me. Every day, each hour. He would reveal a truth in his Word. One I had read a million times, but now it would come to life in a whole new way. He would slow my breaths. He did not grow weary of my coming to him again and again. He never tired of my need for him, of my admitting my fear.

I had to choose to agree with Christ concerning his truth that he declared over me. I had to choose to confess, ask for his help, turn from fear, and turn toward faith. I had to choose to take up my shield of faith and fight in this battle. Yes, the battle continued. But he gave me all I needed to fight and overcome. And he continues to do that today.

We have a choice to choose fear or to choose faith. Sometimes, that choice is a one-time thing, but often it's a day-by-day, sometimes moment-by-moment choice. Will we agree with Christ, or will we agree with lies?

As the apostle John reminds us, "For everyone who has been born of God overcomes the world. And this is the victory that has overcome the world—our faith" (1 John 5:4); while Timothy says, "For God gave us a spirit not of fear but of power and love and self-control" (2 Tim. 1:7).

I am not a fearful person. I am God's daughter and have been given the Spirit of power, love, and a sound mind. I can choose to fight the lies, the thoughts that leave me spiraling, the worries of the unknown or "what-ifs" with his truth. I can stop the downward spiral of my thinking to focus on what he says about his character, his works, and me.

He promises that he is always with me and that I can do all things through Christ who strengthens me (see Phil. 4:13). It may be hard, but God promises to use trials to build my character and hope, and hope never disappoints in Jesus. I might fail, but God's power is made perfect in my weakness.

I want to be a woman of faith, not a woman of fear. I want to be defined for my faith, and I want to live in faith. Because that's who I am in Christ. Given the victory to be faithful in the hard things, in the battles, and to have faith in the One who holds the whole world in his hands and holds my frail, trembling heart too.

Being women of faith doesn't mean we won't *feel* fearful; it means that we won't be defined by fear. It's our doing that brave thing anyway, even if we're shaking, as we rely on Jesus and his power. A lot of our lives will be spent doing the right things, the hard things, *in* our fear. A normal day may require us to surrender and confess our fear every hour. We don't have to grasp for control, and we don't have to conjure up faith on our own. We simply can call out to Jesus and ask him for help.

Jeff is always reminding me that God says over and over in his Word to not fear. He wouldn't say that unless he understood that we are fearful. It's normal to fear. He meets us there. We have to keep running to him. And although that fear may not go away or feel any less frightening, he promises to give us the strength, wisdom, and courage that we need. Being brave doesn't mean we don't feel scared, but rather that we do what needs to be done even when we *feel* scared. For me, that sometimes looks like my leaving the kids while we go on speaking trips, or bringing the whole family along and not knowing what the

next week will look like. Sometimes, it's getting up on that stage or getting on that Zoom call, sweating, and speaking what I feel that the Lord has asked me to say. Sometimes, it's simply getting out of bed for the day and doing what is required of me. I still live scared. But I choose to walk in faith despite my fears. (Well, a lot more than I used to!)

Friends, we are not defined by our fear. We are not worriers who live with low-grade anxiety. We are victorious in Jesus. We are fought for, spoken over, filled with his mighty Spirit. He gives us all we need in life to overcome. We may not think we're overcoming, but moment by moment, day by day, we can choose to try again. We can choose to have self-control over our thoughts. We can choose to run into the safe arms of our Savior and ask for his help. We can walk in faith as we put his truth in the deep storehouses of our hearts. We can fight the good fight of faith as we put on his armor. The helmet of salvation. The sword of the Spirit. The shield of faith. The breastplate of righteousness. The belt of truth. The shoes ready to carry the good news of the gospel.

We are warriors, not victims. And we know how the story ends. We have the victory in Christ. He goes before us, he walks behind, he fills us with his Spirit, and he is with us wherever we go. He is strong in our weakness, faithful in our sufferings, and courageous in the storms. One thought at a time. One moment at a time. One day at a time. His grace does not fail.

So let's fight, friends. Fight well. Fight in faith, in good hope.

Chapter 9

OH, HEY BODY!

For you formed my inward parts;

you knitted me together in my mother's womb.

I praise you, for I am fearfully and wonderfully made.

Wonderful are your works;

my soul knows it very well.

My frame was not hidden from you,

when I was being made in secret,

intricately woven in the depths of the earth.

Your eyes saw my unformed substance;

in your book were written, every one of them,

the days that were formed for me,

when as yet there was none of them.

PSALM 139:13–16

I sat there under a shaded umbrella, taking a day away for rest, my feet up, and my swimsuit on. No makeup, my eyebrows begging to be plucked, messy bun disheveled on top of my head. My feet, although my toenails were freshly painted pink, were rough and calloused and in desperate need of a real pedicure. My belly button was no longer an innie, and the love handles were in full bloom. My bottom was wanting to keep up with my growing belly, and stretch marks were making their claim in places I'd rather not name.

I was approaching my third trimester with Lucy, my fourth pregnancy. I had never struggled with my body changing as much as this time around. I remember when I was pregnant with Kinsley, our first child, how I was in awe of my changing body. I longed for the day when I couldn't see my toes. I took a picture every week to document her growth, so amazed at this new little life growing inside me. I felt nauseous most of the time, but healthy. I couldn't wait to meet this little person, and I was so astonished at how God made our bodies to change and grow life inside us.

When I became pregnant with Kannon, our second, I was incredibly sick and running around like a crazy mama trying to take care of our toddler. I didn't have as much time to think about what my body was doing; I just knew this was what happened and embraced it with full arms.

Then, after Kannon, we lost our Ellie Grace at eight weeks. Having death pass through me was horrifying. I don't think our bodies were meant to do that. My body physically grieved. Very slowly, day by day, month by month, I began to heal.

Months later the plus sign appeared when I was least expecting it. Oh, we had been trying and I had been longing and asking God, but I was too scared to hope again. Even after we found out we were pregnant, it didn't really sink in until twelve weeks, when I felt much more confident that this little life was healthy and growing.

You would think after having two amazing kids, after losing one and grieving deeply and longing so desperately for another, that I would revel every day at this new life inside me. That I would rejoice and be glad and not even think of what I looked like, or the weight I was gaining. Guilt can run deep, can't it? And shame.

I gained weight so quickly with Lucy. One week an outfit would fit, and the next it would be too small. Everything in my closet seemed to have shrunk. I often looked in the mirror and felt anything but pretty. I hated how the words "frumpy," "ugly," and "fat" seemed to scoff at me when I looked into the mirror. My focus was on all the areas that I wished were different.

It was scarring to go to the doctor and have her say, "The amount of weight you gained this last month is concerning." And then to have her question my eating and exercise routine. I remember popping over to a friend's house after an appointment, crying to her about what the doctor said and the weight that seemed to double overnight. It was so hard to stop the doctor's words from running through my head on repeat. To not look down at my body or in the mirror and shake a finger at myself for what was happening. Of having to surrender and let go of feeling I had to control what was happening and living in fear of what I ate and how much (or how little) I exercised. Body image was a years-long battle for me but one where I found victory and freedom. Yes, I was healed from my eating disorder, but it was as if God wanted to free my mind and heal my heart in a different way through this pregnancy. A deeper healing. Another battle. One that was needed not just for me, but for the baby girl I was carrying and for my sweet four-year-old daughter.

My body was changing. No, it was not what it was prepregnancy, and it sure wasn't

what it was on my honeymoon! Parts were bigger and saggier and bulgier. But as I sat on that lounge chair in the shade and watched my tummy move, and felt kicks and high fives, I was reminded of the miracle that was growing inside me. A little baby with a beating heart and strong lungs and legs and muscles and a brain. Ten little toes, ten little fingers. An answer to many, many prayers, and a gift to our family, and to the world. She was worth it. And every time I looked down at that growing belly, I gave thanks and rejoiced, instead of complaining and sinking myself into despair. I wanted to have the eyes of Jesus, to see myself as he saw me. A beautiful woman, a mother, a life-giver. An image-bearer. His holy temple; the place where his Spirit dwelled. To pave the way for my daughters to walk in freedom.

Little Lucy needed more space to grow. I needed more weight to carry her. She ended up being my biggest baby at a whopping nine pounds (with a head circumference in the 97th percentile—in true Bethke form). She has been the only baby we've had with rolls and squishy cheeks and a tummy that sticks out like Pooh Bear. She is the cutest, most adorable little love.

I was discouraged that I struggled so much with my body image while I was pregnant with Lucy. And honestly, now that she is a year old, I've been discouraged that things aren't quite returning back to where they used to be. Granted, I haven't quite signed up for an ab challenge or given up my love for chocolate chips dipped in peanut butter. That pregnancy craving did not leave! My breasts have somehow concaved inward, being a size that isn't even measurable. Let's just say mom jeans are from heaven, and the fact that you can just zip up all that extra is from the Lord. Except when you sit down and have to unzip yourself because, whew! Those be tight!

You may have looked in the mirror today and seen only your flaws, all the things you'd like to change, all the things you'd like to hide. You may have a long list going of all the

things you wish were different, that you could change, that if you just gave up something or completed some challenge you could attain.

But friend, we are so much more than what we see in that mirror. If I were standing with you right now, looking in that mirror with you, I'd say that I see a woman who is beautiful.

Beautiful.
Strong.
Sacrificial.
Courageous.
Hardworking.
Free.
Victorious.
Kind.
Hopeful.
Living.

Your body, all the scars—all the changes for better or for worse—they tell a story. And that story, full of hope and sorrow, pain and redemption, is beautiful in his hands. Perhaps we've been believing the wrong definition of "beauty." Perhaps, it's not at all what we see

in the mirror, but it's all in the heart, as we learn from 1 Samuel 16:7: "For the LORD sees not as man sees: man looks on the outward appearance, but the LORD looks on the heart."

Of course, it matters how we tend to and care for our bodies. They are gifts from the Lord, and we are given the responsibility of keeping them healthy. To feed them. To nourish them with healthy food. To drink lots of water. To exercise in order to work out our stress and emotions and find freedom and peace. To take care of our hearts and lungs and legs. Proverbs 31:17 says, "She dresses herself with strength and makes her arms strong." We need to take care of our bodies because they are in fact the temple of the Holy Spirit who dwells inside us, and we need to be good stewards of his gifts to us. We need to make ourselves strong so we can do the work that he calls us to do. But strength does not look like a certain size, or looking more like *her*, or having those abs you used to have when you were twenty. Strength looks like health. It looks like a woman who can carry heavy loads, who can run marathons, who can climb mountains, who can carry two baskets of folded laundry up the stairs! It looks like carrying your baby nestled to your chest, going on hikes with your kids. It looks like helping your husband with household projects, carrying groceries up to your second-story kitchen, giving a friend a big hug, digging to make a garden. Strength looks like being faithful and steadfast when times get hard, relying on the Lord's power when our weaknesses are laid bare. Strength looks like emptying ourselves and finding refuge in Jesus. Letting him carry us. Surrendering our bodies, all that is and isn't, and seeing our bodies through his lens—how they tell a good story.

Are we women of peace? Of joy? Do we have laugh lines instead of worry lines? Do we glow with God's presence abiding in us? Do we see the blemishes of our bodies as stories that proclaim his goodness?

When we look in the mirror, can we tell ourselves five things we love about our bodies, and give thanks to God, instead of focusing on the five areas we wish were different? Can we give thanks for those areas that we wish were different because we see them in God's light, like larger legs so we can run and hike, or bigger arms so we can carry heavy loads, or a birthmark that is cool because we are the only one who has a mark just like that?

The other day we went surfing at the cove with the kids. It was the first time we had taken the kids surfing, since we've been waiting until Kinsley is a stronger swimmer. And boy, did we get the bug to keep going! Both Kinsley and Lucy went out on the boards, feeling safe with their dad and both being so brave, while Kannon wanted to just play in the waves and hold my hand the entire time. (Of course I will hold your hand, buddy. I know these years are precious and few.) Honestly, I didn't feel superconfident with my body.

My tummy still had rolls, my thighs had stretch marks, and I wished my arms weren't so skinny. But you know what? It didn't matter. I was so thankful to be out in the water with my kids, enjoying that gorgeous ocean, the clear blue sky, and the waves crashing at our feet. I couldn't believe that I got to be there, laughing and making memories with my kids, giving a thumbs-up to the girls every time they caught a wave, giggling with Kannon, and kissing the hunk of a man I call my husband. My kids don't look at me and see my body as imperfect; they look at me and know that I'm their mama, who adores them, plays with them, is intentional with them, and gave them life.

Our bodies are incredible, friends. They have been with us since we entered the world, and they will be with us until we leave. Let's be kind to them. Let's honor them. Let's celebrate them. Let's speak words of life over them. They have been given to us, with all their imperfections, scars, varicose veins, and stretch marks, to serve a purpose. We are here to tell a good story. You are beautiful. Don't wish your body away, but rather embrace it and let it glorify him!

Chapter 10

GARDEN OF
OUR HEARTS

When life is heavy and hard to take,

go off by yourself. Enter the silence.

Bow in prayer. Don't ask questions:

Wait for hope to appear.

Don't run from trouble. Take it full-face.

The "worst" is never the worst.

LAMENTATIONS 3:28–30 MSG

This summer we decided to plant a little garden in our backyard. We started with tomatoes, basil, mint, and sunflowers. I'm slowly learning how to care for these little seeds, and have been amazed at how I can go to the garden every other day and pick fresh tomatoes to pair with eggs in the morning and gather baskets of basil for Jeff's homemade pesto. And I love looking out Jeff's office door at these little sunflowers sprouting up.

My mentor, Robin , once told me that I have a personal Garden of Gethsemane. When hard times come—which they sure do—going to that place is important to me. Having that solitary place to cry out to Jesus and feel all the feels and let him hold me there. That it's okay to go there and cry out to Jesus: I need that. But she also warmly warned me that there's a bridge between me and others, and I must take good care of the bridge to come back and open up to my people and let them walk with me in those hard times, because I can be tempted to cut off all ties to that bridge and turn away from others.

Hearing these prophetic words was healing to my soul. I always knew that when I was distraught about something, it took me extra time to process and cry it out and journal and be alone. And I *somewhat* knew the struggle I had with being totally transparent with my people; or, rather, with pursuing them and being open to sharing all that is in the deep well of my heart when I'm hurting. I've seen how when I'm fearful or upset, I shut down with other people. I can't talk about it, so I run away in a sense. I don't take very good care of my bridge to let people in to help lead me to the truth that sets me free. Especially when it comes to Jeff. We are so transparent in our marriage, but there have been times in the past when my heart was grieving or hurting so much, where my fears had over-whelmed me, that my gut reaction was to cut off all ties. To tear the bridge down, and try to find comfort and safety on my own. It hurt too much to let anyone in and see what I was walking through in the inner parts of my soul.

I feel things deeply and have to run to my Father and spend time with him. I have to cry it out with him and let him hold me. And he always has been faithful to meet with me there. But now I feel permission to do so too. To not do it in hiding, but rather to even ask for it. To have soul care because I know what my heart needs. Sometimes I need time to go off and be by myself and let the tears and pain come and then leave them there at my Father's feet. To gain his insight into it, so I can come back over the bridge and have words to share with those closest to me about what's really going on in my heart and what I need. Why do I feel so fearful? Why am I angry? Why is this so heavy on my heart? And just as Mary sat down at Jesus' feet and listened to his teaching, I also come and listen to him. To my Savior, who is always faithful to reveal what's going on in my heart and how to walk forward in faith and with hope.

Robin has always taught me that our hearts are like gardens. We must be careful to take care of them, and to protect what and who enters in. Perhaps that's why vulnerabil-ity is so hard sometimes. Because we are letting someone into our garden. We're letting them see the weeds that are wrapped around our flowers, the vegetables that have holes from the unwelcome bugs and insects. We know that our garden is precious, and perhaps fragile, and we know the importance of letting in people who will handle our garden with care. Who will understand the preciousness of our fruit and beauty and will love coming in.

Jesus went to a garden on the night of his betrayal. He went to the garden to pray, to cry out to the Lord, to be alone with God when no one else was looking. It's where he met with his Father. And it's where we meet with our Father too. How we tend our garden matters. What we fill our minds with, what we let our eyes see, what we listen to, the peo-ple we surround ourselves with, the people we go to or don't go to when we're struggling; it all matters. Vulnerability with safe people matters. Being open and honest with those we trust is worth the hard work. It's worth it to let them see our dark spots so we can let the light in. Only we know the state of our hearts. Only we know what we hold back and what we let out. And only we can make the decision to cultivate our hearts so that they thrive and flourish.

You, my friend, are unique and operate differently. But no matter how the Lord has wired you, there is something to be said about obscurity, and going off by yourself and meeting with Jesus. Getting away from all the noise and distractions and responsibilities of your days, and simply going and sitting at his feet for a while. Whether that's simply to breathe, or to worship him, to tell him about your day, to pour out your heart to him, to grieve, to mourn, to seek his face. To put down the phone. To stop scrolling. To put off some of your to-dos. To delegate a few tasks. To put on a show for the kids. To have your husband or babysitter or grandparent take the kids for an hour so you can journal your heart out. To go for a walk.

We are not what we do; we are the beloved of God, and as such, he longs to be with us. God longs for our hearts, not our works. Our works are simply an overflow of what he's doing in and through us. Yes, we are commanded to do good works and be on a mission, but that can be done only if we sit with him first. Be with him. Rest here for a while. We are not slaves who are required to constantly produce, but we are his beloved children who are loved and cherished and enjoyed. From that position then, we go out and live on mission out of celebration of what he's done and who he says we are.

We must take care of the garden of our hearts. It's there where Jesus meets us, where he plants fruit, prunes the shrubs, pulls the weeds, waters the soil, shines his light, builds the little chicken coop like Joanna Gaines has in her garden! It's worth it. It's worth taking ten, thirty, sixty minutes to go off and be with him. To take a break from the demands of our day. I feel like I can spiral so fast or dig such a deep trench of sorrow in my heart but keep running on empty because of all that's required of me or, rather, because of the pressures I put on myself. But when I say yes to going off and being myself, I always come back refreshed and renewed with hope. (Usually with puffy eyes, because let's be real: those are the times I can finally let the floodgates open!) We don't have to wait until we have time to go off and be with Jesus, because sometimes that never comes. We have to schedule it in, push things aside to make it a priority. Maybe it's a weekly date with Jesus—a walk, some quiet time at the park, going to the coffee shop and journaling. Or maybe we're in a season that is more demanding, or we're walking through some emotional heaviness, and we need to get away more often to process it all.

There was a season a few years back when life just felt heavy and I was emotionally processing so much. My heart ached; my burdens felt like they were going to be the death of me. So I scheduled a weekly getaway to journal and talk to Jesus. Some weeks, I even got away a few times because I felt so fragile. When the burdens lifted, I realized how much my soul needed that space, especially as an introvert. So I have continued to get away once a week to be with Jesus. So much so that Kannon will often ask me, "Mom, can I go with you? I want to meet Jesus too." Schedule it in, friends. It'll change you.

He has made us with a magnificent garden and wants us to flourish. But we have to do the work. We have to dig the well. We have to take up the shovel and uncover our hurts and sorrows and bitternesses. We have to admit our failures, confess our sins, open our hands that long to grasp for control. We have to till the ground. Plant the seeds. Water the soil.

Colossians 3:15–16 says, "And let the peace of Christ rule in your hearts, to which indeed you were called in one body. And be thankful. Let the word of Christ dwell in you richly, teaching and admonishing one another in all wisdom, singing psalms and hymns and spiritual songs, with thankfulness in your hearts to God."

What's the state of your heart, friend? Overwhelmed? Frustrated? Resentful? Prideful? Go off by yourself. Wait for hope to appear. Hear what he has to say to you. He will speak. He will comfort. He will shine light. He will lead. He is for you and with you. And you will come away with his indefinable peace.

Lately, I've been copying Scripture into a journal for ten minutes each day. I've gone through a few books of the New Testament, and I've been blown away by how such a simple act is producing such great fruit. When I go for my walks and pray, his Word comes to my mind. When I'm talking to a friend, a verse pops into my head to share with them. When I'm struggling to get through my day with joy, or to have hope in a situation, his Word comes to mind and I can recite it out loud. His word is richly dwelling within me. Transforming me. And it's so simple. I'm planting his words in my heart, and they are changing me.

I have to constantly weed out the things that don't help my garden. Music lyrics that get stuck in my head that don't uplift me. Shows that make me feel yucky. Resentful thoughts that start to ricochet in my head like a ping-pong ball. Complaining and grumbling in my heart that go unchecked.

Put on love. Put on thankfulness. Put on praise. Put on truth.

My hope is that we would be women who exude peace, joy, and love. That our lips proclaim his goodness, our hearts hope in him, and that we trust in him. To be known as women who are present and are loved well. But we can do that only when we tend the garden of our hearts. The hard work is worth it. And we have the best Gardener. Oh, what beauty and bounty will unfold as we continue to meet with the Gardener of our souls and let him do his faithful and good work in us. Let's go off into the secret place, quiet the noise, and be with the One who loves us best.

Chapter 11

TRUE IDENTITY

The Lord your God is in your midst,

a mighty one who will save;

he will rejoice over you with gladness;

he will quiet you by his love;

he will exult over you with loud singing.

ZEPHANIAH 3:17

I feel like I've spent my whole life discovering who I really am. What am I passionate about? What motivates me? How am I wired? Why do I react the way I do? What are my gifts? What is my personality like? What is my calling? What boundaries do I need to set in motion to flourish and accomplish that which I'm called to do? What does this season of life look like? Who am I? Who does God say I am? What purpose has he given me? How does he see me? What does he say about me? Who has he uniquely made me to be?

Perhaps we will always be discovering who we are because we're always changing, hopefully growing into our true selves. Our seasons change, our responsibilities change, our limitations change, our weaknesses may be different at different times; we grow, we become, we are. And the more we learn about the Lord, the more we will feel set free in who we are. The more we will feel secure in what he calls us to do, and what our purpose is in our families, our communities, our areas of influence.

In his book *The Gift of Being Yourself*, David Benner writes, "The goal of the spiritual journey is the transformation of self. As we shall see, this requires knowing both our self and God. Both are necessary if we are to discover our true identity as those who are 'in Christ' (2 Corinthians 5:17), because the self is where we meet God. Both are also necessary if we are to live out the uniqueness of our vocation." Becoming our true selves (not in the world's trendy way of "find yourself" that's so popular today), living authentic lives, is wrapped up in knowing God and coming to know ourselves. They go hand in hand. You cannot know one without the other. I realized that I can fully know God only when I know myself because—like Brenner points out—the self is where we meet God. If I don't understand why I do what I do, how can I change at the core? If I don't know how I'm wired, how can I accomplish what he has set forth for me to do in the best way I can? If I don't know my uniqueness, how can I really rejoice in what I bring to the table? And I've found in the world of Christian circles there's two sides we are prone to fall off on. One, and this would be the dominant view I believed growing up, is that the self is bad and self-esteem is horrible and you should never focus on yourself—to do so is wrong. But the other side is just as popular right now if not more so in Christian circles and that's that uninhibited freedom with no restraint is equated with "finding self" and that "being true to yourself" really just means adopting and chasing desires—even the ones that destroy and corrode our soul. But what if (like most things) there's a seed of truth in both, yet tiny land mines that will blow up on us if we aren't careful? That self-awareness, as long as we are asking the Holy Spirit to be the flashlight that is the one doing the illuminating, actually is intertwined with how we come to know God in Jesus. Because becoming our full image-bearing self, should, turn our faces towards the true image-bearer—Jesus.

One week during small group, our assignment was to ask God how he sees us as well as how he sees our friends. Then we gathered together and told each other what we felt the Lord telling us. As we shared, other people could add in anything they felt the Lord had told them about that particular person. It was powerful as I got a glimpse into how the Lord truly sees his body.

Since that night, there have been a handful of other moments when God has spoken to me about who I am in him. The moment always comes when I'm doubting myself, curious about if I should take a certain step, and asking him to speak to me. It never comes in the way I anticipate. Most of the time, my identity words come through my friends. They'll end up voxing me or texting me, saying that when they were praying for me that morning, they felt the Lord give them a word.

Hope bringer.
Prophet for this time.
Strong in his strength.
A pillar.
A willow tree.

These words have been like little love notes from my Father that I keep buried deep in my heart and go to often, to remind myself of how he sees me, of the purpose he's called me to in this time, of who I am in him. The funny thing is, I don't *feel* like any of these things. Most weeks, I find myself discouraged, sad, down, and burdened with something. I have to fight to have hope. I feel fearful of saying the wrong thing, struggle with people-pleasing; and with my soft voice I often give up in a boisterous conversation where I can't get a word in. I am more aware of my limitations and weaknesses than ever and often feel inadequate to complete the task at hand.

But when I feel those things, when I am discouraged with my weaknesses and fears, I remember who God says I am. Of what he calls me to. I can bring hope when I rest in his hope. I can speak a good word when I abide in his words and know confidently that he has spoken to me. I can be strong when I lay my weakness at his feet. I can give thanks for being a pillar in our community of abiding in Jesus and studying his Word. To rejoice at being a willow tree—one who is sensitive, but whom God delights in because I find my nourishment by his waters. My sensitivity can be my biggest weakness, but it also can be powerful when surrendered to Jesus because I am sensitive to what he is doing and what he says and what others feel.

I know I am called to bring hope and to speak truth, all while abiding in him. But how that plays out changes with each season. Sometimes it's writing emails; sometimes it's writing books. Other times it's getting up onstage with my husband, and sometimes it's leading small groups. Sometimes it's praying with a friend, having a conversation with my daughter, making dinner for a new mom, painting a picture for a friend, sharing a word that I feel the Lord spoke to me over someone. My calling looks different, but when I am close to the Father, listening for his voice, for when he says "Go,"

or "Do this," or "Yes," I listen, and sometimes (okay, a lot of times!) trembling, I do what he has asked or confirmed. We must soak ourselves in his Word and sit quietly to hear his voice, to seek him and ask, in order to know who we are and what we are called to do. It takes humility, surrender, openhandedness.

I've realized that giftings naturally pour out of us, even if they still need to be shaped and matured. Sometimes we can't see what our giftings are because they come so easily—"Oh, not everyone enjoys this?"; "Not everyone can do this?" We must speak truth over each other. Tell someone what gifts and abilities we see in them, tell someone when we see them coming alive. Parents, this is especially true for us. Kids shouldn't be left to "go out and find themselves." We have been given the gift, and the responsibility, of bringing out and encouraging the giftings that we see in them, and of leading them in wisdom. Pray over them. Ask God to help us see them as he sees them and speak that over them. Our words matter; they can change the trajectory of lives, for good or bad. We live into what is spoken over us.

God created the world with his words. He spoke, and it came to be! We are not God, but our words matter. Our words shape and form others, and ourselves, for good or bad. One sentence that someone speaks to you can either deeply wound you and take you off course, or build you up and give you wings to fly.

During school recess when I was in second grade, I was swinging on the monkey bars with a couple of girlfriends, and one of the girls said to me, "You're too fat to swing like me." It hurt at the time, but I kept playing and forgot about her comment. It didn't really affect me, and it wasn't something I shared with my mom when I got home that day. Twenty years later, as I was writing a Bible study on finding freedom from body-image issues and telling my story of a six-year battle with anorexia, I remembered that moment on the monkey bars. And I realized that she was the voice I'd heard for years. It was her words that had started my doubts and fears and worries about my body, and one of her words that I shaped my identity around—fat.

Now, it was my choice to believe her words, and I was the one who wrapped myself in those lies for so long. However, it amazed me how such a simple sentence, spoken when I was very young, dramatically affected my life. Words matter.

At the same time, hearing the words "You are a hope bringer," or "You are such a good mom. So patient and intentional and fun," has propelled me into living into those truths. Sometimes I bark at my kids or am mean or demand too much or slide things under the rug that shouldn't be overlooked. But I know that my fear, my worries, my sadness, my bad days and rough moments and fleshly outbursts don't define me. I can recall what has been spoken over me and choose to live into that. As author Sharon Miller wrote, "God spoke realities into existence, and we do the same when we name someone's calling." We have the power to bring life and purpose and hope to others. We have to guard our mouths and speak the truth. To ask God to help us see our kids, our husband, our friends as he sees them and then share that truth with them. It's powerful.

I had been planning a party for a group of sweet friends, and two months beforehand I asked the Lord if he would speak to me about each one of the women who would be in that room. The meetings we had been having throughout the year were coming to a close, and I wanted to give them a special gift as a send-off. I couldn't think of anything greater than sharing an encouraging word.

I sought the Lord so much those two months. I stayed off social media so I wouldn't know what was going on in their lives, and instead truly just heard what God told me about each of the women. I felt him tell me, "Alyssa, of course I will give you a word for these women. They are my daughters and I love them. Of course I will share a loving word."

And he did. I wrote down each one as I felt led. I prayed over every one of them. Each message was nothing but loving, gracious, kind, and warm. Calling them to specific things, but all in love and hope.

I was nervous to share what I felt led to that night. I was sick to my stomach for weeks. The last thing in the world I would want to do is misrepresent the Lord. That night I gathered all of my 5x7 cards that I'd had Jess paint watercolor flowers on. On the other side I had written my note to each woman. I came shaking, and humble.

"I have been asking the Lord for a word for each of you for months now. Wanting to see you as he sees you. I know I'm only human, and not God at all. I do feel like he spoke this over each of you, but please take it with an open hand. Seek him to see its truth. I am simply acting out of obedience and so much love for each of you."

And then I read them. One by one. And as I shared each one out loud, each woman in that room had tears in her eyes. They told me how timely their messages were; how encouraging and hope-filled.

Months later, the words spoken over each lady had played out. It's come to fruition. It's still giving hope. I know that they were touched by those cards that night, and they all sent me a picture of their cards and said how they were thankful. But honestly, I think I was the one who learned the most. What a blessing and honor it is to seek the Lord on behalf of someone else. Of seeing them as he sees them. Wow, that changes my perspective! It certainly takes out all insecurities. It has taught me to know God's voice, to be able to trust when I think he's speaking to me. I learned more about his character, of how truly loving he is, of how his kindness leads us to repentance and conviction and obedience, of how he loves us as a good Father. I learned the power of speaking up and speaking over others. It is a gift we all can hone. To proactively speak truth over our friends, and family. Of speaking words of life and hope.

Friends, we all are saved and set free and beloved in Jesus. But we also are each given unique callings and giftings in him too. Who are you and what does he want to do through you? Ask him to show you how he sees you, and let those words propel you to be the person he made you to be and to do what he has set forth for you to do. We need you! And others need you to speak life over them.

Chapter 12

ENOUGH

But he said to me, "My grace is sufficient for you, for my power is made perfect in weakness." Therefore I will boast all the more gladly of my weaknesses, so that the power of Christ may rest upon me.

2 CORINTHIANS 12:9

On Wednesday mornings we go on field trips with the kids. After we finish our schoolwork, we all pile into the car and go somewhere for the rest of the morning just to get out and explore. On this day, we packed up all the sand toys, made pb&j sandwiches with homemade bread to take along for lunch, and drove to our favorite little spot to play in the tide pools for a few hours.

As I sat on the beach towel, looking out at the crashing waves and blue sky, I talked to God. I felt like I hadn't been a great friend lately because I'd not been as quick as I felt I should have been to support and encourage some close friends who were carrying a heavy burden. I felt like I hadn't been the greatest mom, having gotten frustrated and not been as peaceful or patient as I would like. I had big God-size dreams for business and ministry ventures but was unsure if I could handle them, if I was the right girl for the job. Fear of failure loomed like a foggy June morning. I had negative self-talk about my body and my late-night dessert snacks.

I felt like I was not enough.

Oh, how many times that thought has run through my head and embedded itself in my heart. Honestly, some seasons in my life, that has been my theme song. If I let it, it can sweep me off my feet and bury me in a deep hole. It's such a sensitive topic that the slightest allusion to that from someone else immediately brings tears to my eyes.

I am constantly facing my weaknesses, and it frustrates me. I hate that I can't muster up enough strength and charge into the unknown, into the hard, into the dark.

I'm not one to pull up my sleeves when the going gets rough and say, "Let's do this!" I don't get excited about change or transitions. I don't love surprises. I get discouraged by my limitations; feeling like I can't do it on my own, or hold it all together, or walk it out.

Morning walks help me to get my body moving, to walk out my stress, reorient my wrongly placed energy, and stay mentally healthy. It uplifts my spirit to get outside, to be quiet, to be able to talk with the Lord and process all that is in my heart and swirling around in my head. Every house we've lived in, I have walked around that neighborhood thousands of times, praying and processing and literally walking out my salvation. God has met me in each of those places. He has breathed life into my weary soul, time and time again. It's where I often hear his voice. His convicting of my heart. His leading me to step out in faith and do the work he has for me. It's where I dream, and ask, and give praise. Even so, some days, no matter how hard I fight, I get bullied into believing I'm not enough; that I'm constantly coming up short. I often feel inadequate, overwhelmed.

When Lucy was five months, I started a Bible study called *Mom Set Free* by Jeannie Cunnion, and it was just what I needed. I dug in little by little, because some days with three kids—including a baby who was up at night and a toddler who was potty training—the mornings came sooner than I'd like and often my study time was cut short. I slowly made my way through that study and it completely transformed me. I had no idea of the baggage I'd been carrying around. The pressure I had put on myself to be a *perfect* mama. To hold it all together.

Now, I knew I wasn't perfect. If you had asked me if I thought I should be perfect, or have it all together, I would have told you five reasons why we shouldn't and can't be perfect or have it all together. I knew that was true, but I didn't believe it for my own life. Life with kids throws perfection out the door, and at some stage you learn to roll with the punches. I believed that I needed to be a perfect example to my kids. I wanted to show them Jesus—his unending love for them, his abundant grace. I wanted to always respond with patience and kindness and joy. I wanted them to see Jesus in me, but instead of pointing them to Jesus, I felt the pressure to *be* Jesus. To be more than enough for them. To always respond with patience and kindness and love. To always know what to do, what was the best thing, to be full of wisdom. To not have to ask for forgiveness because I would always do the right thing and respond in the right way.

Through that study, though, I realized this earthshaking truth: I don't need to be enough, and never will be, but my God is. My job is simply to point my children to him, in my weakness, to make much of him. I learned that I don't need to have it all together—which was so freeing because I knew I never would. But rather, pointing my children to Jesus, who would always be enough for them, brought me peace and security.

I am learning the beauty of his strength in my weakness. I can count it a joy to boast that in my weakness, *his* power is made perfect. I am learning that my limitations are a gift and not a curse. They cause me to rely on Jesus, to set firm boundaries, to step out in faith and not let fear drive my decisions, to remember time and time again that I need a Savior.

So when I get impatient, I can ask my kids for forgiveness, and use that opportunity to show them how I need Jesus just like they do. Mom is not perfect, and I need to rely on Jesus every moment of every day. I get an opportunity to share the gospel with them. Of grace and forgiveness. And humility.

When a child isn't listening to my voice, I can ask my almighty God for wisdom to handle the situation, because he tells us to ask, and he will generously give it to me. He knows my child's heart better than I do, and he will show me. When the day's schedule goes haywire, and the baby won't go to sleep and everything seems to be going wrong, I can take a deep breath and ask God to show me how to see him in this day. And ask what

he has for me today. I can rejoice in today, because he is right here with me, faithful to strengthen and equip me; and I can choose to behold him, and step into his cadence and purpose for the day, instead of mine.

God is enough.

And I have God.

Therefore, I have all I need.

He will faithfully give me all that I need for that moment, and that day.

As believers, we are called to live with open hands, surrendered hearts, and to obey. Freedom comes when we lay it all down at God's feet and ask him to guide our steps. When I feel I am not enough, instead of letting those thoughts bury me in self-pity and fear, I can see them as road signs telling me that I need to dig into my thoughts and see where I'm not trusting the Lord, where I'm trying to control and be enough for everyone. I then can turn it over to the Lord again, and ask him to satisfy me with his steadfast love and to rest in his good care of me. I can rejoice in this day, because he goes before me, is with me, and holds it all together.

Armed with this truth, I can wake up with hope. I can face my day with joy. I can take a step forward in faith, trusting his work in and through me and in any situation. I can trust him to provide, to care for me and my family, to guard my heart. I can also say no, or set boundaries or take a step back, knowing that this is exactly what he's calling me to and he will take care of it. I can go on my morning walks to pour out my heart to God and to be in awe of his creation. I can get outside in nature and remind myself of how good he is. He made everything; he sustains it all. It's not up to me. It's in his hands, and here in creation I can breathe deep and release.

We can live free, joy-filled lives when we live surrendered. When we embrace our realities and enter into his rest. God is a God of order and peace, and he has ordained peace for us. He wants us to live lives that are full of love, joy, and peace. But in order to do so, we must surrender and live for the audience of One. We must learn to be comfortable in our weaknesses, to let his power be on display in our lives.

Recently a friend shared how hard this season has been for her, and through tears she admitted, "Sometimes I get so frustrated at the Proverbs 31 woman. She seems to be perfect and able to do it all. I can't do it all. I can't live up to that standard. And then when you look on Instagram, it seems like everyone is able to do it all." And then my other friend, Carly, spoke this truth that will stick with me forever: "Yes, but she didn't do it all at once. Her life was in seasons. Those verses were about different seasons in her life. She grew, learned, did different things at different times. We can't do it all and aren't being asked to. We just need to step into the season God has for us and fully embrace it, frailties and all."

Life is lived in seasons. God does not ask us to do it all. What he asks of us in this current season is to abide in him, to pray, and to find our all in him. He will do the good work through us. He will show his power and might. Our job is to be willing, obedient, and honest. When we let go of the pressures and expectations, embrace our weaknesses, and let his love satisfy us, we can live free and happy lives. No, we can't do it all, and we aren't asked to. Yes, we will fail and let others down, but those are moments to humble ourselves and be reminded of his grace.

My friend, we can step into our day, into our season, into whatever God is calling us to do—whether it's adding or subtracting responsibilities—and walk out in faith, because he is God and we are simply called to live faithfully. In our weaknesses, sometimes crawling on our knees, all the while looking to him. He is delighted in our hearts when we trust through surrender and obey through love. We are enough.

You are enough.

Part III

SMALL THINGS

Abide in me, and I in you. As the branch cannot bear
fruit by itself, unless it abides in the vine, neither can you,
unless you abide in me.

JOHN 15:4

My dad is a man of routine and finds joy in the small things. He loves doing puzzles on the patio, watching *Gunsmoke* daily (he's an old-Western type of guy), and he plays cars with Kannon for hours. He loves Jesus, my mom, his kids, his grandkids. He's the one who taught me that people matter, not things. That cars are simply vehicles to get me from place A to place B. To be like a duck, and let burdens and frustrations roll off my back. He always has a pun ready, as all amazing dads do, and he will belly-laugh until he cries. He has the most tender heart and often tears up when he is sharing a good word with someone. He taught me to get outside and enjoy creation, to play hard and work hard. He has taught me to take joy and delight in the small things, because those are what make up our lives.

The other day I was in the kitchen, rolling up protein balls and listening to worship music. Lucy was next to me, stuffing one ball into her mouth after another, and Kannon was playing with his cars at my feet. Kinsley and Jeff were out spearfishing, and I suddenly was overcome by so much peace, joy, and delight. I couldn't help but smile and thank Jesus for such a sweet moment. But I also was caught off guard. Here I was doing something so mundane and simple, and yet, I was satisfied. I was singing along, happy I could serve my family, and thankful to spend time with my kids. I was working, and yet I was going about it slowly, willing to be interrupted, laughing with my kids. I felt Jesus in that moment, his peace overwhelming me.

It was such a small act of worship, such a small thing in my day, and yet it filled me up for the rest of the week. Perhaps I was so surprised because that moment satisfied me, and yet was countercultural to our current era. We're living in a time that tells us to do more, be better. Its underlying current is to check off the boxes, accomplish the goals, and focus on the *doing*, the *accomplishing*. It falsely promises us that we can do *all* the things, be *all* the things, and that being a success is our destiny. We are swimming in information. If we don't know something, we pull out our phones and google it and in five seconds we have our answer. We scroll social media and are bombarded with messages of how to be more efficient, buy more things, level up. And we are so inspired by what everyone else is doing, we feel the pressure to do it, too, but not just one of the things, but everything that we see. We feel the pressure to be available at all times of the day and night, and to be all things to all people. We can't silence our phones, or shut them down, because what if so-and-so calls, or what if there's an emergency? Or we're waiting for someone to respond back to us.

All these subtle messages bombard us daily. Our culture promises success if we just work hard enough. Social media feeds us the lie that we can have it all if we try hard enough. If she can do it, so should you. It's hard to weed out the truth these days. To still the voices so we can hear the one true Voice that matters. We have to stop the messages that we pick up as we observe others, and instead focus on hearing God's message to us. What is God asking us to do? What is his cadence for our lives? What kind of life did he live? The truth is that we can't be all things to all people. That's omnipresence and only God can do that. Rather, he calls us to a certain place, in a certain time, with certain people around us.

Yes, you have the world at your fingertips, but who is actually in your life? Who do you see on a daily or weekly basis? Who is right in front of you? Or who is the Lord continually putting on your heart? Are they getting your full attention?

May we be focused on bettering our hearts and souls above all else. To continually seek his face, coming before him on our knees, letting him change and transform our hearts. To settle in, abide, and spend time with him before we go out and do. To hear our Shepherd's voice and what he is calling us to do, to focus on.

What does God want me to do today? What does he want me to focus on in this season? What is he calling me to? Not what do I feel pressure to become. Not what do I need to keep up with. Not what is on my to-do list. But what does he want me to be about for his kingdom? As author Ruth Chou Simons says in her book *Beholding and Becoming*, "We become what we behold." What we love is what shapes our lives. Are we loving Jesus above all else, or are we loving success and busyness and control?

God doesn't call us to be the best; he simply calls us to be faithful. To slow down; to rest with him; to abide in his presence. When I focus on doing more, or being better, or being more efficient, I actually feel overwhelmed, that I'm not enough, can't be interrupted, and I'm more focused on the tasks at hand or what I can accomplish than my heart or my kids' hearts or the heartbeat of our home. I lose track of what the Bethkes are about, what God has called us specifically to, of what our unique giftings are, because I'm so busy trying to do it like *they* do, or to be better in that area.

Now, of course we should always be growing and learning—and I hope to do that until my last breath. But when I start to feel my breath quicken, when I start to get short with my kids, or upset that I'm interrupted, I know I'm not living the way Jesus calls me to. I know I've lost sight of the destination because I'm too caught up in making the journey the most efficient and presentable that it can be.

Jesus' words wash me with peace and true lasting joy again and again. He doesn't call me to be successful; he instructs me to be faithful. He doesn't call me to always be available to all people, but he tells me to be fully present and to love people well. He tells me

that hearts are what matters most, not the dishes being put away or the house being put in order or having a delicious meal served hot right at 5 p.m., or my child reading by the time kindergarten is over.

He tells me to sit. To breathe. To surrender and welcome him into my day. Who do I serve today? What do you want me to do today? What things can I let go of on my to-do list? He tells me that his burden is light, and his yoke is easy. That I can hand all my burdens over to him, and walk in step with him. He holds me in the palm of his hand.

Sitting for a few minutes, taking some breaths, lighting a candle, watching the clouds pass by, saying good night to another sunset, painting a watercolor while listening to my favorite album, listening to my kids belly-laugh at their dad's tickles, sitting in the middle of the living room watching my oldest daughter hold and kiss her baby sister, seeing my dad chase the kids around the house, sitting on our couch reading one of the books from Lewis's Chronicles of Narnia during snack time, having the space to text my dearest friend, slowly folding laundry by myself when the kids are asleep, going for a walk to look at the trees and flowers, sitting on the beach to watch the boats sail by, and even sitting alone writing, not anxiously because I'm worried about how much time I really have, but rather with deep breaths, thankful for each moment because I know it's a gift from God. These still, small moments are what satisfies me. They aren't fancy. They aren't necessarily Instagrammable. They're the everyday little moments that make up my life. When they're slow—or not even slow, because sometimes that's impossible with three children—when my heart is slow, when I'm at peace, when I'm abiding in Jesus, when my heart is at rest with him, knowing and believing that he's in control, there is so much joy to be had.

God is among us. He dwells with us. He makes his home with us. When we dwell with him, when we make our home with him—the home of our hearts—we can live lives of joy and peace. To put off the hurry and running about as if we are homeless. When we come home, and stay, remain, abide with him, then our souls are at rest, and we can be fully satisfied, in all the little everyday moments that make up the big ones. Let's not be so focused on the big moments that we rush through the little ones and miss out on the good life God is giving us.

I've learned from my dad that small things are what makes up the big thing. But we miss the small things when we're too busy chasing after the big things, or trying to make the big thing happen. It's about the habits we form that truly shape our lives. What we do with each of the ten-minute sets in our day. What habits are we forming? Are they truly giving us life, or are they prohibiting real joy? Ten minutes can change the trajectory of our lives. A small amount of time, but one that is purposeful and set apart.

Take ten minutes to . . .

* sit and just *be* with Jesus;
* open his Word and read it, or maybe copy some verses down;
* connect with your spouse;
* play whatever your kids want to play with you;
* walk around the neighborhood;
* make a healthy lunch;
* sit around the dining room table and tell stories of any kind;
* facetime a grandparent;
* write an encouraging note to a friend;
* work on a craft or creative outlet that fills you up;
* snuggle your baby without doing anything else; or
* lie in the grass and make up what you see in the clouds.

We can capture the goodness of our lives by being intentional when we enter into all the little moments. Instead of rushing through our days trying to keep up, finish, accomplish, or be better, we can slow down. We can choose to do the best thing. We can choose to prioritize family, connection, peace, delight, loving and serving others, taking care of ourselves. Running through life, trying to do all things, will leave us running on fumes and missing out on the true joy God has for us. It's funny that we talk so much about FOMO, and yet, as we try to live our best lives, we are doing the very thing we fear—missing out on the life God has for us. In every small moment, he is there. Wanting us to receive, to see his presence, to fill up, pour out, live in his cadence.

This is your moment: right here, right now. Not when you finally finish the thing, go on that vacation, accomplish the task, check off the list, complete the ten steps. Right now. Take a mental picture. Soak it up. Breathe. God has only goodness for you.

Chapter 14

LEARNING
CONTENTMENT

> But godliness with contentment is great gain, for we
> brought nothing into the world, and we cannot take
> anything out of the world.
>
> I TIMOTHY 6:6–7

When we moved to Maui we got a forty-foot container to ship all of our things over. It still blows my mind that we live in the middle of the ocean, and so many of our things come by boat! We had been told to buy anything we needed on the mainland and put it in our container before we moved because Maui's shopping and home goods supplies are very limited. (This was before the only Target had been built.) So, I scoured craigslist and found crazy deals on Pottery Barn furniture and shopped my favorite boutiques before we left to stock up on all the cute, farmhouse, beachy finds I could. I kept telling myself, "It's just for our move. Once we get there, I'll have everything I need and will stop spending money."

But after we settled into our new home, painted all the walls and put in new flooring and filled the rooms with our furniture, I kept buying. I kept shopping and found new favorite online stores. I knew something deep in my soul was off, but I didn't want to stop and pull up the rug and see what was underneath. I didn't want to take a good look at the condition of my heart. Frankly, it was hurting. I was so thankful to be living our dream, and for all God had provided, but I was missing home, missing my best friend, and struggling to find friends here. I knew my buying was a reflection of my brokenness, but I just kept on, trying to fill the void with tangible objects. Plus, it was fun. It gave me something to do, something to look forward to.

Shopping had quickly become an unhealthy pastime for me. When I wanted to numb out from a hard day or hard moment with the kids or a fight with my husband, I went to my favorite stores online. When I was down and sad or anxious, I went shopping for a quick fix to feel better. When I was battling loneliness, I found shopping could fill time and give me something to look forward to.

Fast-forward a few years, and I was suddenly faced with my idol. I really see that moment as a mercy of the Lord. I had been spending too much, I hadn't been the best steward with our finances, and God was allowing us to walk through a season of pruning. We needed to be more shrewd with our finances, and so Jeff gave us a challenge: "Let's not spend money on anything that we don't need. If it doesn't fall in the categories of food, electricity, mortgage, or our cars, we can't buy it. I don't know how long it will be, but we need to do this for a time. I believe the Lord is asking us to do this."

I wholeheartedly agreed with Jeff. We needed to do this practically, but I also knew the Lord was wanting to do something in my heart. I knew he was wanting me to find my identity and joy in him and not things.

But the truth was, it sucked. It was almost as if part of me were being stripped away. Shopping was what I did in my spare time, what I loved, what I found happiness in. I loved shopping for our home, for our family, and I loved buying thoughtful gifts for my friends. Nothing was better than finding something that I knew a friend would love.

Have you ever seen *Confessions of a Shopaholic*? Well, in a small way, I was her. Not that I had a closet full of vacuum-sealed designer clothes, but I loved the freedom I had to buy something when I wanted it. Freezing my credit cards felt like an infringement on my freedom. And honestly, it felt like part of my self was having to die.

But slowly, the Lord kept opening my hand. He kept whispering to my heart, "Alyssa, come to me. Come find joy in me. Come learn what contentment is. You have loved money and things more than me. Come to the true fountain of life. I am your true joy."

It was true. I loved Jesus and served him, but deep down I wanted what I wanted when I wanted it, and I felt like I needed those things to be happy. The truth was, I felt like he was withholding good from me. I believed the lie that if I had that one thing, or had the freedom to buy when I wanted to, I would be fulfilled, happy. I was putting my hope, even if it was temporary, in things, instead of him. I was running to things to find my purpose, my happiness, and my healing.

Consumerism is such a normal thing in our culture that often we're blinded to it. It's not so much that we consume, but that we overconsume and are consuming things of this world instead of the Word of God and all that he has for us. Oh yes, it is exciting to get those new shoes or to try out the latest hair accessory or get new pillows! (Ah, I love me

some pillows!) But we know deep in our hearts when our purchases are out of fear or brokenness and not freedom and joy. We know when we're running from something, trying to keep up, or trying to fill up some void.

It doesn't matter what our financial situation is, how much money is in the bank, or how much credit we have on our credit cards. It doesn't matter if we have a little or a lot. Money and things allure us and give us false promises. How true were these words of Jesus: "You cannot serve two masters" (see Matt. 6:24; Luke 16:13). You cannot love money and Jesus; one always wins. The little moments, the small purchases, the "I want it; I need it" thoughts that run through my head, matter. They show what I truly value and treasure.

Are our souls resting in God, knowing that we have all we need in him—in life and godliness? Or do we think that we need more, that he's withholding good from us in some way and that this one thing will bring us the satisfaction we are looking for? Of course, we can shop and buy and spend, but it all comes down to our heart condition. Where is our true treasure?

During this challenge, termites infested our upstairs bathroom, and at the same time, I was itching to create a nursery for Lucy before she was born. At first, I was discouraged that we couldn't immediately get new cabinets for the bathroom or fix up an adorable nursery. But after I started to pray about it, asking God for specific things, for wisdom and provision, I started to get really creative, and thankfulness grew in my heart. I began feeling grateful instead of entitled.

One day Jeff got completely grossed out by the hundreds of dead termites inside our bathroom cabinets (apparently, they have a mating season?). He called up a buddy and they tore them all out and took them to a dump in a matter of two hours! My mom painted, Jeff put some shiplap in, and we bought a new sink and faucet. We were able to use an antique dresser (thanks, Mom!) for our vanity and put in a bookshelf to store towels and baskets. It was amazing to see the needed changes come to life with things we already had!

As far as Lucy's nursery, I prayed and asked God for specific things. Things that I thought seemed a little silly and perhaps were only in my dreams. But he answered them, and this eight-months-pregnant mama shed some good tears over his tender care! Jeff tore out some shelves in the closet, my mom painted the room the sweetest pink, and my parents gifted us the dreamiest chandelier. We already had a crib, and my mom gave us her old rocking chair that she had spent hours upon hours rocking me in growing up (thanks again, Mom!). It's my favorite room in our house! So sweet and pretty, and I cherish all the hours I've spent rocking Lucy to sleep and feeding her in there. I felt so loved and in awe of how mighty my God was by seeing him answer my prayers. Prayers that seemed petty, and yet he said yes. Prayers that made me feel loved and seen and cared for. I loved that I couldn't just go out and buy everything I wanted, but instead was allowed the joy of asking my Father and waiting to see how he answered.

It has been fun to work together with Jeff on these projects, to see God provide and to tap into this creative side. I used to love to craft and create things, but when I became a mom, and we were financially able, it was just easier to buy things. But along the way, I lost the joy of creating and replaced it with consuming.

Since we've done this challenge, I've learned to sew pillows and blankets for the kids, to create farmhouse-style signs that fit our family. I love looking at different pieces in our home and remembering how Jeff and I worked on them together, and thinking, "Wow, we made that." It's sweet that when God shows you your home with new eyes, you start to move things around and things start to feel fresh. "That's where that piece was supposed to be this whole time." Or you realize how you really don't need certain items and removing them makes things simpler. The other day, I wanted something green on a particular shelf, so I went out to my yard and clipped some tropical greenery and put it in one of my favorite vases. It was just what that space needed.

Kinsley read a book a few months ago about a girl who made a dollhouse out of cardboard. It completely inspired her, so we worked together to create her own dollhouse out of a box. We used craft glue to add fabric to the walls, and she colored rugs and carpets and pictures. We cut out doors, put in furniture made of wood scraps, and cut up packing popcorn to be food for her friends. She has a Magnolia dollhouse in her room that she got for her fourth birthday, but you know what? She loves this homemade dollhouse more! She plays with it every day. I love her creativity, and how she made it her own, and the lesson she gave me of how the sweetest

treasures in life are those that can't be bought. And how creativity is birthed through boredom and necessity. What can I use? What do I already have? When we start seeing life like that, it seems that our eyes are opened to God's abundant blessings and gifts.

I enjoy watercoloring and have recently started cutting out little parts of my watercolor flower paintings to use as tags for presents, or as little cards to send to friends. I feel like it makes a present just that much more thoughtful and touching. And it's so simple and free! I love saving ribbon and gift bags to reuse; saving mason jars from pasta sauces to store pantry items or leftovers in. I've relearned what sweet gifts written cards or letters ripped out from notebooks are to friends and loved ones. Praying for a friend, making homemade protein balls, repotting a succulent as a gift, foraging on our family walks—these are all ways I'm learning to be joyfully resourceful.

I still struggle with consuming and often need to check my heart when I want something. The fact is, I love new books and new clothes and home decor. But the Lord has shown me his tender love, his faithful provisions, and has led me through a journey of making sure I treasure him more than things. Is he my all-in-all? Do I turn to him to truly satisfy my longings? Do I rely on him, or do I try to do it all myself? Am I buying something to fill a void, or is it out of contentment and joy? Our hearts are actually longing for Jesus, and he's so much closer than we realize. Jesus tells us that he will fill our every longing and his love is what satisfies. Everything else will fall short, will "satisfy" for only a limited time. We'll be faced with the temptation to want more. But with Jesus, there are no limits. He satisfies, truly, and continues to give more and more.

As Chris Tomlin sings, may we be a generation that seeks his face above all else, a generation of people who have "clean hands" and "pure hearts" and do "not lift our souls to another."

Satisfied

Chapter 15

LAUGHTER

A cheerful heart is good medicine.

PROVERBS 17:22 NLT

Growing up, whenever my mom made lasagna, it would take her all day to simmer the red sauce, layer the noodles, and gather all the ingredients. Lasagna seemed so decadent and special that when my childhood best friend, Renee, and her husband, Jon, came to visit us in Maui, I wanted to make it for them. I had been slowly cooking each recipe in the book *Bread & Wine* by Shauna Niequist, and she had a lasagna recipe that looked fairly easy and somewhat healthy. Now, I never really read through recipe instructions before I make them. I see one I like, glance over it to make sure I have all the ingredients (okay, most of them), and go for it. And for some reason, I always think it's a good idea to try out something new when we're having guests. It's kinda chaotic and stressful and perfectly coincides with my type B personality. (And that is the complete opposite of Jeff, who studies videos before he makes anything, and always tests out a recipe before guests come—at least once, if not twice!)

So I gathered the ingredients and went to work. I dreamed of a special evening with our friends sitting around the table, having a heart-to-heart conversation and a delicious dinner. I wanted them to feel loved and served. Being around the table is a high value in our home. Even if it's not fancy, I love gathering my people and nourishing their stomachs as well as their hearts. There's something special about a table and food. It brings people together, opens conversations, and breaks down walls in ways that other settings can't. It makes people feel loved and accepted and wanted. It's a tangible way to show the love of Jesus. And I love thinking of who is coming over and providing them with yummy food that they can eat. We have so many memories of people being gathered around our table throughout the years, and I remember the conversations, the feelings, and the food—whether it was good or bad!

I worked all afternoon to put the lasagna together while the kids napped, set the table out on our lanai overlooking the ocean, and waited excitedly for our friends to get home from their excursions. We all sat down to eat, the sun shining through the shades, bowed our heads to pray, and then I dished up the lasagna.

"Mmm, this smells so good, Alyssa."

"Thanks so much for dinner. You did not have to do that."

We all took bites, and it was silent for a bit. Well, not that silent. You could hear loud cracking and chewing and crunching. I spit my mouthful out. Renee chewed as fast as she could and swallowed hard, swigging it down with a big sip of water. Jon just sat there smiling and chewing.

Jeff cleared his throat and asked, "Are you sure it's done all the way?"

"Yes, I cooked it for the time it said. Why are all the noodles so crunchy?! I followed the recipe exactly."

"It's not bad, really. It's good. Has great flavor," Renee said.

Jeff picked around the lasagna to discover that none of the noodles had cooked. They were just as crunchy as when I had taken them out of the box.

140

Satisfied

I was horrified. "Why didn't the noodles cook? I don't get it. I got 'oven-ready' noodles just like the recipe called for. The box said you didn't have to cook them first, you could just put them in as is and they'd cook in the oven."

"Well…"

"They're definitely not cooked!"

Jon just kept taking bites of his crunchy lasagna and eating with a smile on his face.

Renee took another bite. "It really isn't bad, Alyssa. Just kinda crunchy."

Jeff dug in and ate away, peeling off all the noodles and eating just the sauce and meat.

I quietly pushed my plate away, feeling like a total failure. All I wanted to do was make my friends a special meal that was delicious and have a special night of sharing our hearts. Instead, it was a disaster.

"I'm so sorry, guys! What a failure!"

Renee ate slowly. And Jon finished his piece off. Renee cut him another serving and placed it on his plate. He took another bite.

Crunch. Crunch. Crunch.

Renee let out a slow rumble of laughter. Jon started laughing through his bites. Jeff lost it too. I couldn't help but belly-laugh as well.

"Alyssa, it's actually good. Jon loves it! He doesn't mind the crunch!"

And somehow, we ended up eating the whole lasagna—Jeff picking out all the noodles, Jon crunching away, and all of us laughing with tears in our eyes for the rest of the meal.

Every time I remember that night, I start to giggle. Who makes a crunchy lasagna? Oh, this girl right here! And whose friends just laugh and eat the whole thing anyway? My sweet friends. No, it wasn't what I had planned. I don't remember having any deep conversations that night, but I remember the joy, the love, the grace, and the laughter. And isn't that what I wanted the whole time? To be filled with joy, connect, and share a memory? It is one of my favorite memories around the table. Seeing their smiles, laughing until it hurt.

The other day I heard a statistic that kids laugh four hundred times a day, while adults laugh only fifteen times. While I'm unsure how accurate that is, I do know my kids laugh all throughout the day, and I want to be more like them. I want to be full of joy and laughter too. Two of the many blessings that children give us are joy and laughter. Finding so much joy in the smallest things. Seeing all the little things, and being in awe of them. Being fully present in the moments God gives us.

Let's be intentional about finding ways to be joyful. We can turn up the music and sing at the top of our lungs. We can have a random dance party with our kids. Kiss our husband out of the blue. Write a sweet note saying you love them and see them. We can say yes to that nap. Take up a pencil and doodle something pretty. We can have cake for our midafternoon snack, or make a delicious salad for our lunch because it's important to feed our bodies good food too. We can take a leisurely bath, jump into the pool with the kids, have a water fight, Nerf gun fight, play hide-and-seek. We can take up a paintbrush, plant a new vegetable, go for a walk with our family. We can have a bonfire and sing songs, or have a dinner party and share hearts. We can play a board game with friends, do a puppet show, lie on our backs and watch the clouds move across the sky. We can make popcorn and watch a movie, build a fort, take a friend or one of our children on a date. Paint our nails, put on facial masks, go feed ducks, go to the library, slide down the slide with our kids. Text that friend and pursue time with them, or plan the gathering you've been wanting to host forever.

We can say yes to fun, to spontaneity, and to joy just by living surrendered, available, open lives. Living slow enough to say yes, to clear our plates so we can put the good stuff on them. The spontaneous, life-giving things. Saying yes to making fun memories with our kids. Creating space for joy and laughter out of the ordinary goodness in our day. Laughing when things don't turn out exactly the way we expected.

Sometimes things simply do not go as planned. You go to all this trouble to plan the perfect day or evening or event or dinner, and life happens. Kids still have tantrums and accidents. You squabble with your spouse. The house gets messy, your dog eats the bread you set out for sandwiches, you burn the rice and undercook the lasagna noodles, you forget where you put your keys, you drive to work with your coffee mug on the roof of your car, or mother-in-law's birthday cake caves in the middle.

Life is never going to be perfect. And most of the time, it never meets our ideal. But that's the beauty of life. The not-so-perfect is usually better than what it would be if it had been perfect. The unexpected surprises us with joy. The hard makes us lean into Jesus. The messy makes someone feel welcome. The letting down of our walls lets someone come in and be themselves. You crack up with your family when you find the keys in the freezer. Your mother-in-law loves her "one-of-a-kind" cake. And your new coworker feels safe talking to you.

There is so much joy in life if we trust in Jesus. Because it's not about the end result. It's not about having it all pulled together beautifully. Rather, it's about declaring his goodness and his faithfulness through our weaknesses. It's not about the finish line, or how our lives look to others. It's about the process of living through the hardships. It does something to change us. It makes us stronger. Forces us to keep going. To ask God to help and give us his eyes to see the joy instead of white-knuckling it and trying to force life to be as it is in our minds. To let go, to trust the process, and lean into him.

We can learn the practice of rejoicing and celebration and happiness. It is a practice, isn't it? It certainly doesn't come naturally all the time. Often I base my joy on my feelings, which is always a faulty thing to do. I am learning and having to resurrender all the time, to let my thinking control my emotions, not my feelings. A huge part of residing in joy is surrendering and embracing the chaos of our lives.

Let's be women who show up for our realities. Who show up with arms wide and welcome in whatever God has for us today. Who welcome spontaneity. Who live like Jesus and welcome the interruptions instead of fighting against them. Who wake up in the morning and say, "Lord, whatever you have for me today, I want to step into it with an open heart. Ready to receive. Ready to laugh and hope and be full of the joy you abundantly give each day because I have you. And nothing can separate me from your love or from your kingdom. You are always my Father; I am always your daughter. You are mine and I am yours. May I see you today and be fully present in each moment." We cannot control the outcomes or circumstances of our days. It's what we do, how we respond to our current realities, that matters. Will we respond with joy?

Chapter 16

THANKFUL HEARTS

It is good to give thanks to the LORD,

to sing praises to your name, O Most High.

PSALM 92:1

Luke 2, which tells the story of Jesus' birth, is one of my favorite chapters in the Gospels. I've always loved how a host of angels comes to the shepherds, some of the lowliest people in that time. Shepherds were unseen by many; they worked out in the country and were dirty and smelly. And then one night, a huge host of angels appears to them, singing and telling them the Savior has been born! The shepherds go see the baby, and when they get there, they tell Mary and Joseph how the angels appeared and told them of the birth of Jesus. It goes on to say, "And all who heard it wondered at what the shepherds told them. But Mary treasured up all these things, pondering them in her heart. And the shepherds returned, glorifying and praising God for all they had heard and seen, as it had been told them" (Luke 2:18–20).

I always stop and think of verse 19: "But Mary treasured up all these things, pondering them in her heart." This verse pulls back the curtain and shows us a mother's heart. Many times I have felt like Mary and have stopped to treasure up things in my heart. Things that the Lord has told me. Things that the kids have told me. Things that are happening around me. A Bible verse. Looking at the ocean or stopping to behold a beautiful flower. Or when I think I'm seeing the Lord work in a specific way that I've been praying through.

We women store things in our hearts. We hold on to things. We are treasure seekers and like to gather all the special things and keep them close in our hearts. I love combing the beach for beautiful shells, or walking through a field and foraging for the

unexpected. My friends and I love finding special treasures at antique stores and displaying them in our homes. Just as we go looking for physical treasures, so we treasure up beauty and truth in our hearts.

The trouble is, most of the time we are gathering the wrong treasures. We forget to look for the treasure and instead settle for the clutter. The things that distract and weigh us down. Instead of going out to collect true treasure, we take home a bunch of fake and cheap things and pile those up in our hearts, making them cluttered and messy. Mulling over our disappointments and dreading the things that haven't happened yet. Collecting lies and storing bitterness. Grumbling and complaining. We focus on the treasures we don't have, instead of all that we do. We fill up our treasure chests with junk, and then distract ourselves or push the hard and heavy things down so we don't have to deal with them. There have been plenty of times when I have had a nagging or complaining thought about my husband simmer on the stove of my mind, to then overflow a few days later at something not even related. We need to look through our disappointments and grievances and bitterness, the things that aren't and perhaps won't be, and deal with them in order to get to the other side. We have to face our problems and emotions and real thoughts head on, so that we can get to other side of healing and hope, truth and grace.

Our thoughts really do control everything. What is filling, consuming, and running through our minds? What do we choose to think about and focus on? What we think about is what we store in our hearts, and what will eventually be visible to those around us, good or bad. And as women, I believe we have the power to either make a space (our home, family, workspace) full of life and hope and joy, or make a space that brings everyone down. How we set the mood and respond to life greatly impacts those in our lives.

The other day I felt cranky and put out and was impatient with the kids. I was tired of having to repeat myself;

I was over the whining and complaining and finally sat them down and gently talked to them. However, the next morning as I was reading my Bible and *Loving the Little Years* by Rachel Jankovic, I was convicted that *I* was the one who needed the heart change. Now, I'm not saying the weight of how our kids respond to life falls entirely on us. We each are responsible for our own actions, but I am saying that we must lead by example. And that day, I certainly did not. Oh, I thought I was keeping it in check, but in truth, my brain was firing on all cylinders with impatience. While we sat down for breakfast, I apologized to them and asked them to forgive me. I wasn't living in joy, and I was guilty of grumbling, and I wanted to lead so much better. They were sweetly gracious and kind with me.

One of the most important ways we can control our thoughts is by regularly giving thanks. It's no wonder that "give thanks" is mentioned seventy-three times in the Bible. In fact, 1 Thessalonians 5:18 says, "Give thanks in all circumstances; for this is the will of God in Christ Jesus for you." It's God's will for us to give thanks.

God knows our hearts. He knows how easy it is to let our minds wander to things that

don't uplift or satisfy. He tells us to take every thought captive to make it obedient to Christ (see 2 Cor. 10:5) and to think on all that is lovely and pure and true (see Phil. 4:8). There are many ways to do so, but the quickest way for me to put off thoughts that are not true or thoughts that are not lovely is to give thanks. The quickest way to end grumbling and complaining (which I am so guilty of!) is to stop and name a few things that I'm grateful for. To choose joy in the moment.

My friend Carly was sharing with me that one day her son spilled a whole container of cheese in the kitchen (this was right when COVID-19 was spreading and we were all on lockdown, and emotions were already a bit shaky as we all adjusted to a new normal and accepted the unknown). And she realized this one truth, which I have been chewing on for weeks now. She was saying to herself, "Oh great. Now I have to clean up this cheese." But then she stopped and realized, "No, I *get* to clean up this cheese." And that changed everything.

Giving thanks.

Choosing joy.

In the moments of inconveniences, messes, frustrations. Bringing beauty out of something that is ordinary or even annoying. She had a son to clean up after. She had cheese to clean up. She had a kitchen floor to wipe clean.

We don't *have* to.

We *get* to.

I get to pick up my husband's boxers from the floor (lying right next to the hamper?!) every day. (Every. Day. Friends!) I get to wipe a runny nose. I get to change a dirty diaper. I get to take out the trash. I get to pay the bills. I get to vacuum. I get to mediate sibling rivalry. I get to have the hard conversation in order to find healing. I get to. What a blessing!

One day, several years ago, I was at my friend Jill's beautiful, beachy, cottage-style house. I'd always loved going to her house. It felt welcoming and full of peace. I was in the kitchen when I saw a journal laid open on the counter, with the numbers 75 through 90 written down the page, and her beautiful handwriting filling up each line. Next to her journal was Ann Voskamp's book *One Thousand Gifts*. My friend was walking through a very difficult season, and to help her find joy and peace, she was stopping throughout her day to write something she was thankful for. It was giving her hope to carry on.

I think of that moment often. This is the woman I want to become. A woman who actively gives thanks. Who stops to write it down because she knows that this one simple practice will dramatically change her. It changes her heart. It changes her thinking. When we give thanks, we take our eyes off all that causes us anxiety, including our fears and

the things that weigh us down, and it gives us wings to fly. Giving thanks fills us with hope and peace because we are focusing on what is true and beautiful. We are seeing God's goodness to us in that very moment. We are welcoming in the presence of the Holy Spirit, and, therefore, we can be a presence of joy to others.

The thing is, God doesn't tell us to give thanks only when our lives are good and pleasant and going exactly the way we want. Rather, he tells us to give thanks in *all* circumstances. No matter what season we find ourselves in, no matter what hardships we face or what healing we're working through, no matter what the doctor's diagnosis or how our children behave or what our checkbooks say or if our businesses are successful, we are commanded to give thanks. No matter what time of month (girl, I feel ya!), what is said to us, how so-and-so responds, or if we feel seen and noticed, we are commanded to give thanks. But I believe that's because there is always something to give thanks for. God is always showering us with his loving affection and his grace. He is good to us, friends! His goodness spills over. And giving thanks is what gives us the eyes to see just that.

The psalmist says, "Surely goodness and mercy shall follow me all the days of my life" (Ps. 23:6). His goodness is pursuing us, but we have to practice giving thanks, to work out our thankful muscles, in order to see it.

The kids and I started playing a new game recently. It's just like I Spy, but you say something you're thankful for. For instance, "I'm thankful for something that's blue and you can swim in it." "The ocean!" "Yes!" It's been a fun way for us to practice giving thanks, and to take a moment to look for real treasure that God has given us.

Let's be careful with what we put in our treasure chests, and let's store up all that is lovely and excellent. Let's see how far we can get in our list of things that we are thankful for.

"What's up, Lu?" said Edmund — and then suddenly broke off and made a noise like "Ow!"

"What on earth—" began Peter, and then he too suddenly changed what he had been going to say. Instead, he said, "Susan, let go! What are you doing? Where are you dragging me to?"

"I'm not touching you," said Susan. "Someone is pulling me. Oh — oh — oh – stop it!"

Everyone noticed that all the others' faces had gone very white.

"I felt just the same," said Edmund in a breathless voice. "As if I were being dragged along. A most frightful pulling – ugh! It's beginning again."

"Me too," said Lucy. "Oh, I can't bear it."

"Look sharp!" shouted Edmund. "All catch hands and keep together. This is magic – I can tell by the feeling. Quick!"

"Yes," said Susan. "Hold hands. Oh, I do wish it would stop – oh!"

Next moment the luggage, the seat, the platform, and the station had completely vanished. The four children, holding hands and panting, found themselves standing in a woody place – such a woody place that ... were sticking into them and there was hardly room to move. ...hes were sticking into them and took a deep breath.

"Not me," said Lucy. "Mine were in my little bag,"

"So were mine," said Susan.

"Mine are in my coat pocket, there on the beach," said Peter. "That'll be two lunches among four. This isn't going to be such fun."

"At present," said Lucy, "I want something to drink more than something to eat."

Everyone else now felt thirsty, as one usually is after wading in salt water under a hot sun.

"It's like being shipwrecked," remarked Edmund. "In the books they always find springs of clear, fresh water on the island. We'd better go and look for them."

"Does that mean we have to go back into all that thick wood?" said Susan.

"Not a bit of it," said Peter. "If there are streams they're bound to come down to the sea, and if we walk along the beach we're bound to come to them."

They all now waded back and went first across the smooth, wet sand and then up to the dry, crumbly sand that sticks to one's toes, and began putting on their shoes and socks. Edmund and Lucy wanted to leave them behind and do their exploring with bare feet, but Susan said this would be a mad thing to do. "We might never find them again," she pointed out, "and we shall want them if we're still here when night comes and it begins to be cold."

When they were dressed again they set out along the shore with the sea on their left hand and the wood on their right. Except for an occasional ... The wood was so thick and tangled that ... thing in it moved – not a bird, ...

Chapter 17

JOY IN THE GRIND

*And let us not grow weary of doing good, for in due season
we will reap, if we do not give up.*

GALATIANS 6:9

A while back Jeff was asked to be a speaker during a Caribbean cruise hosted by *FamilyLife Today*. As compensation they invited him to bring the whole family, including my parents! You know we jumped at the chance. We had a blast, and the kids lived it up. Every day they made their rounds through the splash pad, hot tub, arcade, kids' center, and ice cream bar. At one point we overheard the kids ordering their own lemonades. One day at lunch, when the waitress offered another scoop of ice cream, they said, "Of course."

Jeff and I needed the vacation more than we knew. We were due to speak in South Carolina two weeks later, so instead of flying all the way back to Maui we decided to extend our trip and made our way up to Georgia and South Carolina. We explored and played and talked and slept and rested and laughed. But more than anything, we felt the Lord pouring into us.

I didn't realize how exhausted I was—mind, body, and soul—until we sailed away from Florida. Suddenly, it all caught up to me, and I was depleted. During the first two weeks of our trip, I felt like the Lord just wanted me to rest. To sleep and read and be and heal. Then, finally, during the second half, I felt my soul come back to life and I was able to dream and vision and plan for the next season. I felt the Lord's tender care so tangibly.

When we were on our cruise, Jeff took the kids often to play and eat ice cream, and to let me rest on our balcony. I spent a lot of time praying, journaling, and reading. And I started to realize, as I felt the Spirit searching my heart, that I was entering a new stage of my life. I was officially leaving my twenties behind (although technically

I'd done that a couple of years before), and was now entering the stage of responsibilities. I honestly felt discouraged by how ordinary and mundane my life felt. I was coming to grips with my limitations and was realizing that life is lived as we learn to hold sorrow in one hand and joy in the other. We had exciting things planned and future trips and business plans, but most of my days in this season felt the same. Wake up, get the kids ready, make breakfast, homeschool, play, pick up, lunch, quiet time, work, pick up, make dinner, play, pick up, put kids down, and rest. (Oh, and pick up some more!) Not every day looked the same certainly. Some nights Jeff and I connected and dreamed or went on a date. We would see friends and have people over for dinner and go on adventures. But I was coming out of a season of having to say no a lot, in order to say yes to my kids, my husband, and my emotional health, and I actually didn't know what the next year would look like. The previous year included a lot of loss, and the hope of new, exciting things wasn't yet on the horizon. It just felt the same and all so ordinary. I felt a little stuck.

The honeymoon phase was over—with my husband, yes, but also in other areas of our lives. Jeff and I had been married for seven years. We were well settled into doing life together and fighting against the temptation to just be roommates. We had three beautiful children who required much of our energy and love and wisdom and care. We had businesses and ministries that we were committed to and working hard for. We were settled into our community. The newness of moving and finding friends had faded, and we found ourselves well aware of pitfalls, conflicts, weaknesses that our community (us included!) held. God had blessed us with so much, and with those blessings came an immense amount of responsibility. It wasn't so much about the dreamy "when" or "I hope one day," but now those things were set in motion and we were learning to stay in it, to be steady and committed and faithful.

There weren't big peaks or mountaintop moments anymore, although we always have those in some way throughout our months and years when we're looking with eyes of faith to see God work and move. We can still dream and pursue and hope and ask God to do big things, but we were fully aware of our lives being lived in the everyday, mundane, ordinary moments.

And if I'm honest, it was hard. Most days it looked like the same thing, leaning into uncomfortable moments, accepting the stretching and sanctifying circumstances. Asking God for more grace, extra patience, joy.

My twenties now seemed to have been full of excitement, but those moments were a thing of the past. Like us, most of our friends had settled into careers, communities, families, marriages. The newness had worn off. The steady journey had begun.

When I was sitting on that cruise ship balcony, I grieved the loss of what was. I was disillusioned, disappointed, and depleted by this new stage of life. I looked ahead and it didn't seem exciting—and that scared me a bit. It almost felt boring. Not that I was bored, because my life was so full, but boring in the sense that the shiny and new had faded.

Author Ronald Rolheiser in his book *Sacred Fire* makes an argument that there are three stages of Christian discipleship—essential discipleship, which is the struggle to get our lives together; mature discipleship, which is the struggle to give our lives away; and radical discipleship, which is the struggle to give our deaths away.

For most of my twenties, I was in the essential discipleship stage. For some, that can last until their fifties depending on their life circumstances and decisions. Not to say that we earn a badge if we quickly finish this first step. It just is.

Now I was moving into mature discipleship, which is usually the longest period in our lives. It can involve having a family but doesn't have to. We give to our jobs, to our communities, to our family members, to our aging parents. For me, I had found an amazing man to marry who loves and serves and leads me well; the Lord has graciously given me four children (one in heaven); we have a home; and we are faithful in our work, even though it seems to be changing and morphing every month! And as good as my life is, and so many of my dreams have come true (how crazy is it that God has answered so many of my desires with a yes!), some days I feel exhausted by all my responsibilities. I can become resentful of constantly giving.

If we were sitting on my couch under blankets and sharing a charcuterie board, I would quietly admit to you that some days I just don't want to give anymore. That, honestly, I'd like to receive. I'd tell you how I sometimes long for the stage of life that felt so exciting and held so much anticipation and when, most days, my heart felt much lighter. I felt more like a kid, without so many of life's burdens.

It is a struggle to give my life away. Do you feel it too? I want to be a good friend. I want to be a loyal daughter. I want to be an intentional and fun and gracious mom. I want to be a cheerleader and best friend to my husband. I want to give to others, to encourage

them and spur them on and fulfill God's calling over my life, however that looks in each season.

We are called to give. To give our lives away. And even though it's exhausting at times, and in some seasons, it feels unbalanced when it's not reciprocated in kind. But the truth is, our giving, and the fight it takes to keep giving, to keep laying down our lives, to keep pushing forward in hope and sacrificing, to keep showing up and saying yes and demonstrating grace; the constant and steady faithfulness; this is the good, sanctifying, growing, maturing work. This is the sowing that is needed in order to become mature women who selflessly love others and radiate with his joy. This sacrifice is producing beautiful fruit in us. We are moment by moment and day by day being stripped of our flesh, our selfishness, and learning to become more and more like Jesus, who gave his life away for us.

This long, big, important season of our lives is meant for us to learn to give our lives away and in so doing, to become more like Christ. How could we not savor that? How could we not relish in the fruit that is being produced in us as we give again and again?

Jesus said in John 15:13, "Greater love has no one than this, that someone lay down his life for his friends." Jesus gave his whole life for us, so that we may have life. Likewise, giving our lives away is the greatest act for those around us. Often it is not seen or noticed or thanked. It is not newsworthy. We don't earn awards for making yet another meal for our families and thus preventing our kids from starving. This is not elementary school where we received awards for handwriting or being most inspirational. We don't earn five stars on our chart for cleaning the toilet (although we should!). People don't applaud us for showing up and completing another full day of work or getting up at night to comfort a child who had a nightmare.

But God sees us. God notices. And God has given us this work not only to find delight in, but also to complete his good work in us. God never told us we needed to be successful. He told us to be faithful. And it's in the faithfulness that we are successful. Success in the kingdom of God doesn't look like earning a certain income or reaching a certain goal. It doesn't look like the accolades that our world applauds, or even our Christian circles put on display. Success in the kingdom is showing up, surrendering, saying yes to whatever God lays on our hearts and what his Word says. Success is pouring out. Giving, again. Being the one to lead, to pray for that person, to write that note, to text that friend and see how they're doing.

Success is folding another basket of laundry, making another dinner, saying yes to playing with your kids and laughing with them as you enter their world and share in their joy. Success is listening, being available for your people. Success is staying in God's word, fighting lies with his truth, doing battle in your mind to think on what's true and lovely. Success is admitting your need for Jesus, again. Admitting your fear, again. Success is being honest about your sins and shortcomings and weaknesses and asking God to come and help and comfort. Success is pursuing your husband, opening your heart to him, and not shutting him out or treating him like a roommate. Success is taking care of your body with exercise and water and nutrition. Success is waking up and trying again. Success is saying, "I'm sorry." Success is having the hard conversation. Success is staying in it. As your full self. Being faithful. Steady. Dependable. Putting in the work.

It's easy to feel unseen in the constant giving and serving, in the silence and the ordinary. But in the unseen is where we will do the most important work. I believe in the unseen is where God does his greatest work in us. It's where the fruit of the Spirit is built into us.

Love. Learning to want what's best for the other.

Joy. Despite our circumstances. Anchoring to God's goodness.

Peace. Despite the unknown and scary and stormy trials of life.

Patience. Oh, how we learn patience as we learn to do life with others, show grace again and again and again—with others and ourselves.

Kindness. To be the bigger person and exude his love even when others are not kind to us. Learning to hold our tongues. Learning to give grace.

Goodness. Finding the good, doing what's right, giving good to others.

Faithfulness. Remaining. Steady. Especially when it feels ordinary and the newness has worn off and it's hard.

Gentleness. Learning to control our anger. To speak with kindness on our tongues.

Self-control. Saying no to the flesh and yes to the Spirit. Laying down our lives and serving others.

It's easy to grow weary in this season. We are in it for the long haul. It feels a little deflating to think of this being it until we are near our deaths! But friends, God promises us that he is producing fruit in this. Yes, he will produce fruit in our work and businesses as we continue to show up, do the work, and do it well. He will produce fruit in our kids as we continue to be present, listen, shepherd their hearts, teach them manners and how to solve math problems and read and share with their friends and work through big-heart things like loneliness and friendships and integrity. He will produce the fruit in our marriages as we continue to serve our spouses and cheer them on and pray for them. He will produce the fruit. We don't have to. We simply have to be faithful. To stay openhearted. And give. And as Shelly Giglio said once at If:Lead, "I'd rather be found faithful than fruitful. The fruit is wonderful, but when people talk about me when I'm gone, I'd rather have them say how I was faithful, than to name off all that I did in his name."

And God will most definitely produce the fruit in our hearts. He will mature us. He will make us more like him. He will chisel away our selfishness, our self-pity, our impatience, our pride. Being committed, staying faithful, that is good stuff. That is holy work.

So, as we face one more load of laundry, one more sink piled full of dirty dishes, another week of work, another week of homeschooling, another hard conversation with our spouse, another friendship that may feel a bit one-way right now, another ministry that requires a lot from us, let us choose joy. Joy in the grind. Joy to endure and to persevere and say yes and show up. Joy because this, this is the good holy work that God has for us. It is not boring or mundane or something we should wish away. Rather, let's receive this gift. Learn to do the hard, holy work. Lean into Christ to be our strength and joy. Root ourselves in his love and his acceptance so that we can pour out. Ask the Holy Spirit to come and fill us up, because he never asks us to do it by ourselves. He never asks us to muster up the strength on our own. To find the joy outside of himself. He asks us to come. To receive. To pour out. To give. Because in giving, we are being made into our true, best selves.

I hope that one day, as we move into Rolheiser's stage 3 of radical discipleship, we will be a bunch of old ladies who can sit around a table together, telling stories of our loved ones and how God has been faithful to us, good to us, our true Joy through all of life's ups and downs and in-betweens. I hope that we can look back on this maturing stage and see it as such a gift and a time where we fully embraced the good work he was doing in us. That we all have the afterglow—the true glow of one who has been through it all, who has come out knowing Jesus intimately, and who can't wait to be fully with him. That we will be women who have found our deep satisfaction in the Lord, in his good work in us, and in the gifts that he has given us each and every day.

Chapter 18

MY PEOPLE

How good and pleasant it is

when God's people live together in unity!

PSALM 133:1 NIV

We met in our friend's backyard for a potluck dinner and a worship evening while the sun set. Many friends whom I love and do life with were gathered together. We lifted hands, prayed together, and sang as our kids played quietly and the babies crawled around.

Toward the end of the night, three of the little girls came out to the center of the lawn in their princess dresses and started to dance with one another. As they danced to the music they held hands, smiling big, and twirled with each other. Elsa, Anna, Cinderella. They spun around with such delight, not concerned about who was watching, but simply loving one another, enjoying the music, and letting their little hearts dance with the joy that was in them. Kinsley joined in and started dancing in her board shorts, her long hair flowing behind her. Eventually some of the boys jumped in, and they all held hands and laughed and giggled through the last songs. Kinsley had the happiest look on her face, and she kept wanting to hold her friend Ace's hand, feeling welcomed and safe with him.

Some of us mamas stood on the outskirts with big smiles. Tears gathered in my eyes watching these little girls dance around without a care in the world. They didn't care that everyone was looking at them, or that they couldn't keep a beat, or that they kept tripping in their plastic high heels. They didn't feel like they had to be dressed a certain way, or be a princess, to join in on the fun. Some danced with a partner, while others did their own little jig. But when it was time to all join hands and run in a circle, everyone offered a hand and they did it together. They danced with joy, abandonment, and delight. As I watched them, my mama heart so full, I couldn't help thinking of our hearts as women, how the Lord sees us, and how we are called to be sisters in Christ.

When God sees us, he sees his precious daughters whom he adores and delights in and gives his full attention. And as our Father, he loves us because he loves us, not because of anything we do. He loves us when we're in our pajamas at 2 p.m., messy bun, no makeup, tired from the day and still trying to clean; just as much as when we have to muster up strength to take the kids to the park and then get dinner going; just as much as when we're up at the crack of dawn, on our knees praying and praising him. He loves us when we're delighting in him and doing our work with joy, just as much as when we're stressed out and overwhelmed and wondering how in the world we're ever going to do what has to be done. He loves us when we're preaching truth to our hearts, and when we are overcome by the lies. His love never changes. His love never diminishes. He loves us regardless of how "successful" we become to the world, how much we check off our to-do lists, and how much we accomplish. If we spend the day getting the house all cleaned and feeding everyone and actually putting makeup on and looking great and loving our people well; or if we sit on the couch and do nothing and nurse our baby in our pjs and the house is messy and the fridge is empty and the laundry is heaped on the floor, he loves us still. He loves us when we gripe at our husbands, and when we get impatient with our kids. He loves us always, forever. And he delights in us, always.

God is inviting us into the dance circle. He wants us to hop in and join hands with our sisters. To dance and sing out loud, regardless of what we wear or what we look like or what we accomplish. All that we long for, he offers. He makes us beautiful. He frees us from our fears. He calls us lovely and accepted. He will never reject or forsake us. We will never be too much for him. We will never be too _____ (fill in the blank: emotional, sensitive, weird, different, etc.) for him.

But rather he delights in our uniquenesses and the ways he has wired us, because we each have a role in the kingdom. Yes, he will renew our weaknesses and grow us and shave off our imperfections, but the "thing" that makes us unique is what we need in the circle. We are warrior women who are called to do his good work. We are brave and free and courageous and so very loved.

Oftentimes, we let our insecurities and the past get in the way of joy and happiness and being part of the sisterhood. We think we're too much, or that we don't have anything to offer, or that we're not enough. We aren't like *her*, so we can't join in.

But we are honored and blessed and called and wanted. *You* are honored and blessed and called and wanted. And we need you. The truth is we will never be enough. But we don't need to be. God is enough. And he will infuse us with himself and his Spirit and fill up all that we lack.

Joy filled my heart when I witnessed Kinsley being accepted into that circle of friends. Just as each one of the kids in the circle are unique and have their own passions and giftings, so does Kinsley. And her uniqueness is just what that circle needs. For such a time as this, she was created to be here and be part of these friendships. We need her nurturing, strong, smart, logical, and helpful heart. Her intuition of what others are feeling and need is a gift; her joy for life and her fearless, adventurous spirit bring life to all of us. I am so glad the Lord made her as he did. I love seeing her continue to bloom into the woman God has purposed her to be.

When we show up just as we are, with all that is unique about us and makes us, us, we bring a depth and added puzzle pieces to the group. You were created, dear friend, to live where you live, to be a part of the community you are a part of, to have the family you have, to have the unique giftings and passions and capabilities that you have. Not only are you favored, but you are also needed.

The other day I met up with a few of my best friends for a girls' day. We shared everything that was going on in our lives, prayed for and celebrated each other. As I sat there, my heart rejoiced that God had brought these friends into my life. These are the friends who have cared for us on multiple occasions of sickness, grief, and loss. These are the friends who have come to every birthday party hosted at our house, every holiday dinner and family gathering. They've helped provide for our needs, have seen me cry more than I would like to admit. They pray over me, check in with me, and remind me of truth. They randomly leave flowers or coffees or homemade bread on our doorstep. They throw us parties when we have something to celebrate, say yes to all-day beach days, and come over to help us move furniture around in our house! These people are the real deal. They show up. They love well.

The beginning of our Maui journey brought so much loneliness, but now after years of investing, pursuing, being vulnerable, and continuing to say yes, the Lord has brought sweet friendships into my life. Women who know me, who know my struggles and my fears and my hopes. Women who cheer me on, celebrate me, and go into battle with me.

Regardless of your season, it can be difficult to find good friends. Insecurities rear their ugly head. Time can be illusive; distance can make it difficult; having that one moment where you feel like you actually connect and aren't trying so hard is a challenge. Knowing who you are and being confident in it can seem like an impossible task, especially when you go through a big transition like welcoming a new baby, moving into a new home, finding a new job. Finding your one girlfriend to do life with is like finding a diamond in the rough.

Friends and community are a God-given desire. We are made for them. We need one another. A lot of times relationships are not perfect or necessarily how we envision them, because people are messy and life can be full and busy. It's a lot of work to be a good wife, mama, grandma, employee, and friend.

But here's what I know to be true: First, God is the only One who can fill your loneliness. No person, no girlfriend can do it. That simply puts an impossible pressure on someone else. God alone can comfort you, fill you up, and satisfy you. It's only from a place of resting in God and his love for you that you can be a good friend to begin with. To love someone else well, to have courage to pursue friendships, you first have to be filled up with his love. He wants to satisfy you. He wants to be the One you run to and confide in.

Second, God wants us to have friends. He wants us to be a good friend. He longs for us to be in community. We can't give up. We must keep asking and waiting on him to bring us a friend. And we must keep being courageous. Keep being brave in asking someone to get together. Sign up for a Bible study. Start a prayer group or a workout group. Ask a woman to show you how to make something that they're good at and you want to learn. Throw a party, have someone over for lunch, or go for a walk together. It can be anything. Sometimes it's taking baby steps, or just continuing to put one foot in front of the other.

You may plan something to get to know the people around you and not come away with a best friend, and that's okay. That was certainly my experience. I hosted a moms' gathering for a few months after moving to Maui and felt like everyone else got really close except me since I was often busy with putting it together. However, they loved it so much, they wanted to keep getting together after that, for dinners, another Bible study, Christmas parties, girls' nights. We started a co-op together for our preschool kids, and each gathering, each moment of connection, brought me closer to these women until eventually true friendships were made.

Kannon's fourth birthday was during COVID-19 when we were sheltering in place, and although he understood about not being able to see his friends and their families, deep down my mama's heart was sad that he was missing out on his birthday. Then, at 11 a.m., I got a text for us to come out to our front lawn, and suddenly we heard loud music, honking, and yelling. One by one our friends drove by in their cars, balloons and posters hanging out of their windows. Bubbles were blown, gifts were tossed. Kannon looked at me and asked, "Mom, is this all for me?"

I had been crying the entire time, and with tears running down my cheeks, I choked out, "Yes, buddy. It's all for you. They love you so much!"

Our friend Ian, who is part owner of one of the car dealerships here, had a bunch of his guys drive souped-up trucks for Kannon's parade, too, knowing how much Kannon loves trucks and monster cars.

Real community. Abounding love. People who walk with you in the valleys, and on the mountaintops. Friends who show up. Who give, serve, listen. Who remind you of truth and encourage you. Friends who want to make memories with you and help process your life. My friends have shown me Jesus. They have reminded me of his truth and helped me to fight off discouragement and fear. They have made me laugh and have given tons of grace. Grace when I've needed to step back; grace when I haven't given enough. Grace when I've had to say no, and grace when I couldn't make it happen. They've been honest and spoke up when I've been in the wrong, when I've needed to change my thinking and narrative. They've helped me with the practical and the spiritual.

Don't give up, friend, if you're still looking for your people. God is at work. Not only is he going to provide a girlfriend for you, but he is at work in you! He is building in you a brave spirit, breaking down lies of rejection, making you more and more secure in him, and forcing you to wait and trust in him. The waiting is so hard, but he is at work.

Recipes

ABOUT THE RECIPES

We Bethkes love to eat, but even more, we love to gather friends and family and neighbors around our table and share a meal together. It's our daily rhythm for our family that keeps us grounded and connected, and it's the place where we make memories. There's something about eating food and sitting across the table from someone that makes you feel safe. We've laughed until tears are running down our faces, had kids running around the table with kazoos and party hats, sung songs and blown out tons of birthday candles. We've also shared our deepest pains, fears, and struggles with our people at our table. It is a place that we truly get satisfied, body and soul.

And so I wanted to compile some of my favorite recipes here that share sweet memories for me and will hopefully foster gatherings in your home, at which you can not only satisfy others, but also come away satisfied yourself. Satisfied with good food, good friendships, good conversations, and good memories.

Overnight Oats

I learned early on that toast for breakfast was a joke to Jeff! (But also, if you know my husband, you know that he eats more than anyone I've met. It's as if he's still eating like his nineteen-year-old baseball-playing college self! I mean, if our friends have us over for dinner, they know to make extra!) So we always have a hot breakfast. However, when we had our third baby, serving up a special breakfast every morning just wasn't possible. But we still need something filling and full of protein. Say hello to overnight oats. It's a favorite in our family. I like it cold, since it's summer all year long here, but Jeff likes his hot, so he heats his up before he eats it. The best part is that it takes just 5 minutes or so to prep the night before, and then you're all ready the next morning. (And if I had to be out the door early in the mornings, or rush everyone to school, this would be our breakfast every day! You could totally eat it in the car or on the go.)

Rolled oats

Powdered peanut butter

Collagen powder, nutmeg, and/or cinnamon (optional)

Raisins

Milk (we love oat milk or macadamia nut milk)

For each serving: Scoop ½ cup oats into a mason jar. Take a spoonful of peanut butter powder and place on top of the oats. Add collagen powder and spices if you like. Add a handful of raisins. Then pour 1 cup milk over the mixture, put the lid on, and shake to combine. Refrigerate overnight, or for up to 3 days.

Serve warm or cold. We love adding a bit of maple syrup, fresh berries, or bananas, and sometimes sliced almonds.

Mimi's Summer Salad

My mom is the queen of salads. We had one with almost every dinner growing up, usually just a simple green salad with ranch dressing. But this one was always my favorite. It reminds me of summer in Washington growing up, girlfriends gathered around a table on our patio. Laughing. Sharing hearts. Talking until the sun would finally set late at night.

¼ cup seasoned rice vinegar

2 tablespoons olive oil

2 tablespoons sugar

1 avocado, pitted, peeled, and cut into bite-size pieces

1 orange, peeled and cut into bite-size pieces

1 apple, cored and cut into bite-size pieces

2 green onions, thinly sliced

Lettuce, cut into bite-size pieces

¼ cup Craisins

¼ cup Candied Pecans for Khristine (see page 180) or store-bought sugared pecans

¼ cup feta cheese (optional)

In a large bowl, combine the vinegar, olive oil, and sugar.

Add the avocado, orange, apple, and green onions to the dressing, toss, and let sit in the refrigerator for 1 hour.

Just before serving, add the lettuce, Craisins, pecans, and feta, if using, and toss with everything else.

Candied Pecans for Khristine

MAKES THREE 16-OUNCE MASON JARS

I always think of my amazing mother-in-law, Khristine, when I make these because every Christmas she asks for the recipe so she can make them for her coworkers and friends. Khristine raised Jeff as a single mom, with grit and humility and so much sacrifice. She is discerning and puts her whole heart into everything she does.

These make awesome little gifts—hand them out to your neighbors, add them to a gift basket, or put a little "thinking of you" note on them. They are a pantry staple in our house. We enjoy them alone, or I chop them up and put them on top of pancakes or in oatmeal. But my favorite way to serve them is on top of a yummy salad (see pages 179 and 181). Whenever I pull these out of the oven, whoever is in the kitchen always sneaks a little bite. They're just that good. Enjoy!

½ cup (1 stick) unsalted butter

¾ cup packed brown sugar

1 tablespoon vanilla

¼ teaspoon salt

16 ounces pecans

Preheat the oven to 325°F. Line a baking sheet with a piece of parchment paper.

Melt the butter in a large saucepan over medium-low heat. Add the brown sugar, vanilla, and salt. Cook, stirring for 1 minute, then remove from the heat. Continue stirring until the brown sugar dissolves. Throw in the pecans and stir until they're all coated.

Spread the pecans on the baking sheet and bake for 20 minutes, stirring halfway through, until golden brown.

Remove from the oven and let cool. Store in an airtight container at room temperature for up to 1 month.

Barb's Sweet Salad

We have people over for dinner a lot, and we often grill meat of some kind. I just add a delicious salad and a side to make an easy meal. This is my go-to salad, so chances are if you come over for dinner you will be served this! Everyone loves it, including the kids. Barb, the mom of my best friend Shannon, is an amazing cook, and this is one of her famous salads. It's refreshing, simple, and goes great with most dishes.

DRESSING

¼ cup vegetable oil

2 tablespoons apple cider vinegar

2 tablespoons sugar

SALAD

Spring mix lettuce

¼ cup Candied Pecans for Khristine (page 180) or store-bought sugared pecans or sugared sliced almonds

½ cup sliced strawberries

¼ cup blackberries

For the dressing: Throw all the ingredients in a little jar and shake to combine. Set aside.

For the salad: Place the lettuce in a large bowl and add the rest of the salad ingredients. Pour on the dressing and toss right before you serve.

Jeff's Pesto

Store-bought pesto can be too salty, too garlicky, or too oily. But homemade pesto is so easy, and so delicious. This one is the dreamiest, and I guarantee that you will love it. The best part is that there is a lot of room to substitute depending on your food allergies or budget. Basil is one of the few things I have been able to grow where we live (oh hey, hot weather!) and I'm so thankful because this pesto is on our menu at least once a week, if not more! A jar makes the perfect gift, a great way of saying, "I'm thinking of you, here's some dinner for whenever you need it this week." Pour it on pasta, spread it on bread, put it in paninis. Serve it hot or cold. You can even freeze it.

4 cups packed fresh basil leaves

2 cups cashews

⅔ cup olive oil

Juice of 1 large lemon (5 tablespoons)

½ cup grated Parmesan cheese (optional)

½ teaspoon salt

½ teaspoon minced garlic (1 to 2 cloves)

Place all the ingredients in a food processor and blend until well mixed. Place in 16-ounce mason jar to store; it will keep in the refrigerator for up to 1 week. You can also store in the freezer and have on hand for an easy pasta dish or a marinade. If it's difficult to blend, add a dash of water.

Nicole's Steak Salad

MAKES 6 TO 8 SERVINGS

My friends threw me a dreamy baby shower under twinkly lights one night when I was pregnant with Lucy. Charcuterie boards, lanterns, pink Anthropologie plates, and gorgeous bouquets of wildflowers. We sat around the table talking about all things babies, and they each took turns encouraging me with kind words of what they love about me being a mom. It was a night that I will forever cherish. We had hearty salads, fresh bread, and a chocolate peanut butter cake. Also on the menu that night was Nicole's steak salad. We laughed as she told us how she made the tortilla strips the day before, and when she got home later that day, she found her husband chomping away on them, thanking her for the snack. Whenever I think of my baby shower, and the first month with our precious Lucy, I think of this salad. Nicole also delivered it to us for dinner while we got used to being a family of five. It's delicious. Colorful. And makes for a great party dish. And what really puts it over the top is our friend Jori's dressing, which also is great on almost any salad! Note that you'll need two taco seasoning packets: one packet for the steak, plus another tablespoon for the tortilla strips.

STEAK
1 pound flank steak
Olive oil
1 (1-ounce) taco seasoning packet

TORTILLA STRIPS
8 tortillas, cut into thin small strips
1 tablespoon taco seasoning
1 tablespoon olive oil

JORI'S DRESSING
½ cup apple cider vinegar
3 tablespoons ume plum vinegar (or red wine vinegar)
2 cups fresh cilantro leaves
¼ to ½ avocado
2 to 4 cloves garlic, peeled and minced
½ teaspoon pepper
¾ cup olive oil, plus more to taste

For the steak: Rub the steak with a drizzle of olive oil and the taco seasoning and marinate in the fridge for at least an hour.

For the tortilla strips: Preheat the oven to 350°F. Line a baking sheet with parchment paper.

In a bowl, toss the tortilla strips with the taco seasoning and olive oil, making sure all the strips are well coated. Spread on the baking sheet and bake for 10 to 15 minutes, until crisp. Keep an eye on them because they can burn easily! Set aside. (You can make this a few days ahead.)

For the dressing: In a food processor, combine the cider vinegar, plum vinegar, cilantro, avocado, garlic, and pepper. Blend. With the processor running, slowly add the olive oil until well blended. If it's too vinegary for you, add up to ¼ cup more olive oil.

Preheat a grill to high heat. Cook the steak, turning once or twice, to desired doneness, and let it rest for 10 minutes. Slice the steak into long, thin pieces.

SALAD

2 heads romaine lettuce, cut into bite-
 size pieces

1 avocado, pitted, peeled, and sliced

1 cup cooked black beans

1 cup cherry tomatoes

1 cup fresh cilantro leaves, chopped

1 cup canned corn, drained

3 hard-boiled eggs, sliced

1 cup crumbled cojita cheese

For the salad: Place the lettuce in a large bowl and arrange the steak and all the remaining ingredients on top. I like to lay out the toppings next to each other for presentation, but you could totally just toss it too! Serve the dressing on the side.

Jeff's Popcorn

MAKES 6 BOWLFULS

Early on in our marriage, we became popcorn people. I think part of it was that Jeff decided to become vegan on our honeymoon. I didn't know much about cooking, let alone vegan recipes! But my husband is an all-or-nothing guy who gets a vision for something and then passionately seeks it out. So we were vegan for the first 6 months of marriage. (Until one day he went through the McDonald's drive-through. It was all over after that!) We loved binge-watching Netflix at night after a full day of work. (*Parenthood* was our jam.) And the perfect snack was popcorn.

It's still a staple in our house for Saturday movie nights, read-alouds, and an easy throw-together snack when friends come over and I don't have a chance to make a dessert or appetizer. When we had twenty people in our home who were evacuating from the fires last spring, I raided my kitchen for things to feed them. After serving up a quick Dutch-oven taco soup, I made a few batches of popcorn for everyone to fill up on.

Jeff usually is the popcorn pro at our home, but every now and then I'll throw a bowl together too. Here's our popcorn recipe.

1 heaping spoonful coconut oil

½ cup unpopped popcorn kernels (The type of popcorn makes a difference! Our favorite is Amish Country baby white popcorn, available on Amazon.)

Salt

Nutritional yeast (optional)

Place the coconut oil in a large skillet over medium heat, along with a few kernels. Cover with a lid and wait until the pan heats up. As soon as those few kernels start popping, add the rest of the kernels (careful not to burn yourself!), place the lid back on, and shake the pan off the burner for 30 seconds. Put it back on the burner and continue to shake it back and forth over the heat until all the kernels have popped, about 5 minutes.

Pour into a bowl and sprinkle salt all over until it tastes just as you'd like! You can add nutritional yeast on top if you want a kind of cheesy taste.

My friend Shanny once told me that she loves a glass of orange juice with her popcorn, and now I always crave it when I eat popcorn too!

Shannon's Tortellini Soup

Years ago, Jeff and I took a trip to the mainland and had just flown into Seattle to spend a few days with my best friend. It had been a long travel day, and we were exhausted and cold. Shannon wasn't home from work yet, but she told us to make ourselves at home and to feel free to dig into dinner. When we got to her house, there was a pot of this soup on the stove and a loaf of sourdough bread waiting for us at the table. We got all dished up, sat at the table, and downed our meal. I have never felt more welcomed and cared for. To have hot soup waiting for us when we got there?! Since that day, this soup has been my favorite and one I make often, especially in the winter. Everyone loves it. It's so comforting and simple, and also super easy to make ahead and freeze. It's the best "welcome to our home, I'm so glad you're here" soup.

3 tablespoons olive oil

1 package sweet Italian sausage (about 1¼ pounds or 5 sausage links), broken up

1 tablespoon minced garlic

1 small white onion, diced

1 red bell pepper, cored and diced

2 to 3 zucchinis, diced

1½ tablespoons Italian seasoning

2 (32-ounce) cartons chicken stock

2 (14.5-ounce) cans diced tomatoes, undrained

1 cup grated Parmesan cheese, plus more for serving (optional)

1 (20-ounce) package tortellini (frozen or fresh)

Handful of spinach

Heat 1 tablespoon of the olive oil in a large skillet over medium-high heat. Add the sausage and cook until no longer pink all the way through. Set aside. (I like to pat mine with a paper towel to remove excess grease.)

Add the remaining 2 tablespoons olive oil and garlic to a stockpot or large saucepan over medium-high heat and let it heat up. Add the onion, red pepper, and zucchini and cook, stirring occasionally, until softened, 5 to 7 minutes. Add the Italian seasoning, stir to mix well, and cook for 5 to 6 minutes.

Add the cooked sausage, along with the stock and diced tomatoes. If you like, throw in grated Parmesan cheese (totally yummy without if you are dairy free). Bring to a simmer. The longer you simmer the soup, the better, but let it go for at least 30 minutes. Always best if you can cook this in the late morning and let simmer throughout the day.

Cook the tortellini according to package directions. (I like to keep my tortellini separate from the soup so they don't get soggy.) Right before you're ready to serve, throw the spinach into the soup. Add a handful of tortellini to each serving bowl and ladle the soup over.

Garnish with additional Parmesan if using and serve with a hot loaf of sourdough bread and butter.

Jeff's Pico-de-Guac

MAKES 3 CUPS

When I was a high school intern at my church in Maui in my twenties, Leslie, one of my friends (and mentors), was in love with the Pioneer Woman. Well, one afternoon after a hot beach day, Leslie brought over all the ingredients for the Pioneer Woman's guacamole. She chopped and diced and stirred and I've never tasted anything as delicious as that guacamole on that hot July day. (Top it off with a cold mojito or LaCroix and it's golden.) I wrote the recipe down and shared it with my parents when I moved back home. It became a staple.

When Jeff and I got married, we honeymooned in Portland—which was pretty magical—for a little city feel, and then went down to Cancún for a week. We bought some groceries, thinking we'd need to save our money, but really only bought coffee and chips and guacamole supplies. I mean, sweet love can live off guacamole and coffee, right?! I made that recipe for Jeff the first day, and he downed the whole thing and asked for more! (Something about guacamole and chips during summer, or in the sunshine.) We then found out the hotel gave us a generous gift card to be used for the restaurants at the hotel that week, and so we dined liked royalty. But at every meal, we got guacamole. And we still made it in our hotel room once a day. So much so that when I think of our honeymoon, I immediately correlate it with this dish!

It's since been adapted and changed and Jeff has taken over the role of making it since he really does it best. (Or at least I make him think so, so I don't have to make it!) He swears by the three greens: avocado, cilantro, and lime. But if you don't like cilantro, you can really get away without it—just don't tell Jeff I said that!

3 avocados, pitted, peeled, and cut into bite-size pieces

1 large tomato, cored and cut into little pieces (or I like to use a handful of cherry tomatoes)

¼ red onion, finely chopped

Fresh chopped cilantro, to your liking

Juice of 1 lime (about 2 tablespoons)

Salt to taste

Smash the avocado in a bowl. Then gently fold in the tomatoes and red onion. Add the cilantro, lime juice, and salt and stir. Serve with your favorite tortilla chips!

Chicken Pot Pie

MAKES 5 SERVINGS

I never grew up on chicken pot pie, although pie has always been near and dear to my heart. But this year, after we found out my dad had cancer, my dear friend Sarah brought me and my mom multiple dinners as we grieved, and her chicken pot pie was a constant. Not only did I feel loved by her thoughtfulness to make dinner for our family in such a hard time, I also felt the warmth of this comfort food. Now every time I eat it, I am reminded of how Sarah walked through such a deep valley with me, praying with me and holding my hand through it all. She helped me to hope when I had a hard time hoping myself. I loved it so much that I started a quest to find the perfect chicken pot pie recipe for our family. Since last winter, this has been on our menu at least once a month. Every time I make it, I make two, so I can freeze one for later or give to a friend. I love having freezer meals on hand, and this one is so easy.

I made this for my grandparents when they came to visit, and as we sat around the table eating and talking about their visit, my ninety-year-old grandpa, Freddy Bear, declared, "This is the best chicken pot pie I've ever had!" So I hope it warms your heart as it has mine, and Freddy Bear's!

PIE DOUGH (SEE NOTE)

¼ teaspoon salt

2 cups all-purpose flour, plus more for rolling

⅔ cup + 2 tablespoons shortening

8 to 10 tablespoons cold water

For the dough: In a large bowl, mix the salt into the flour. Add the shortening and, with two knives, act like you're cutting the flour and shortening together over and over until the shortening looks like little peas. Slowly add water, 2 tablespoons at a time, stirring with a spoon after each addition, until the dough combines. You don't want to overdo the water, so pour a bit, then stir or use your hands to see if the dough sticks together. Once it is mostly sticking together, take the dough out and form into a ball with your hands. Cut the ball into two pieces and set one aside.

Sprinkle flour on your work surface. Place one piece of dough on the flour, and sprinkle more flour on top, then flatten the dough with your hands. Roll out the dough to make a 9-inch round. Transfer the round to a 9-inch pie pan. (To move the dough, I like to take the round and fold it in half, then in half again, then unfold it in the pie pan. If the dough is too soft and sticking to the work surface, I use a spatula to help transfer it.) Fit the dough into the pie pan.

(continued)

FILLING

4 tablespoons unsalted butter

1 pound boneless organic chicken thighs, cut into bite-size pieces

1 cup sliced carrots (I've used frozen before, and they work great!)

½ cup sliced celery

¼ cup chopped yellow onion

¾ teaspoon salt

½ teaspoon garlic powder

½ teaspoon dried thyme

¼ teaspoon pepper

¼ cup all-purpose flour

½ cup canned coconut milk

1 cup chicken stock

1 tablespoon chopped fresh parsley

½ cup frozen peas (optional)

For the pie filling: Melt the butter in a large skillet over medium heat. Add the chicken, carrots, celery, onion, salt, garlic powder, thyme, and pepper. Cook, stirring often, until the chicken is cooked through, 8 to 10 minutes. Sprinkle on the flour and stir until you don't see any flour. Slowly stir in the coconut milk, then the chicken stock. Cook, stirring often, until bubbling and thick, about 3 to 5 minutes.

Remove from the heat. Stir in the parsley, and the peas, if using. Let cool for 15 to 30 minutes.

Preheat the oven to 425°F.

Scoop the filling into the pie crust.

Roll out the other half of the dough to a 9-inch round and place on top. Pinch together the edges of the dough to complete the pie. Make five little slits on top to let the pie breathe while it cooks.

Before placing in the oven, I recommend placing some foil over the edge of the pie so the crust doesn't over-cook. Bake the pot pie for 30 minutes, until the dough is golden brown. Let cool for 15 minutes before serving.

To freeze, wrap the raw, assembled pie and place in the freezer; or bake it, let it cool, and then wrap and freeze. Either way, make sure to wrap it well so it doesn't get freezer burn. If baking from frozen, unwrap and place the pie directly in the oven from the freezer; bake at 375°F for 1 hour and 15 minutes.

NOTE: This is the best pie dough I've found and rely on. If it seems daunting, or you'd like to simplify the recipe, feel free to buy a pie crust!

Jenna's Artichoke Dip

MAKES 2½ CUPS

My sweet friend Jenna—a master at photography and nutrition and a pillar of peace and love—brought this vegan artichoke dip to one of our girls' nights. I shyly scraped my rice cracker across the top of the dip, and then proceeded to eat a third of it while I chatted with a friend. It is so good! It's always requested at every girls' night, and whenever I make it for a gathering, it gets devoured. Plus, it's so easy and healthy! Serve it up with rice crackers, bread, pita chips, or tortilla chips.

¾ cup milk (I usually use almond milk)

¾ cup raw cashews (unsoaked)

Juice of 1 lemon (3 tablespoons)

2 cloves garlic, peeled

¾ teaspoon salt

Dash of pepper

2 cups fresh spinach

2 (14-ounce) cans artichokes, drained

Preheat the oven to 425°F.

In a food processor, combine the milk, cashews, lemon juice, garlic, salt, and pepper and blend until smooth. Pulse in the spinach and artichokes. Spread in a 9-inch pie plate and bake for 20 minutes, until lightly brown on top and bubbling.

Sarah's Curry

Years ago I held a moms' study group with some ladies from my community, and after it was done, we still longed to gather and encourage each other, so once a month we met for dinner. All of us had different dietary needs, so thinking of a "theme" for dinner was a little tricky. Sarah hosted one night, and made a big ol' pot of curry and it was the most yummy meal. I still remember eating it as we sat around a candlelit table, sharing hearts and asking deep questions.

This recipe is delicious and feeds an army. It's a great meal to serve guests, to take to a family, or just to have on hand. It can also be frozen. This is a great meal option to make ahead of time and have on the stove so when guests come over, your dinner is made and you can rest and enjoy the company.

3 tablespoons coconut oil

1 small onion, diced

2 teaspoons finely chopped fresh ginger

1½ to 2 pounds boneless organic chicken (I prefer thighs), chopped into 1-inch chunks

2 (14-ounce) cans coconut milk

1 cup water (or 1 additional can of coconut milk)

2 to 3 tablespoons yellow curry powder (to taste)

2 red bell peppers, cored and sliced

2 large sweet potatoes, peeled and chopped

4 to 5 small carrots, chopped

Juice of 1 lime (about 2 tablespoons)

2 teaspoons fish sauce

2 tablespoons sugar

Heat the coconut oil in a large heavy-bottomed pot over medium heat. Add the onion and ginger and sauté until fragrant and translucent, about 2 minutes.

Add the chicken and sear until not quite cooked through, about 8 minutes. Add the coconut milk and water, then stir in the curry powder. Next, add the red peppers, sweet potatoes, and carrots. Bring to a boil then reduce the heat to a simmer and cook until the sweet potatoes are tender, about 10 minutes. Stir in the lime juice, fish sauce, and sugar.

Serve over white jasmine rice.

NOTE: To make it vegetarian, simply omit the chicken. You also could use broccoli to replace it, but it's good as is.

Enjoy!

Mimi's Strawberry Cake

MAKES 12 SERVINGS

This is our family's favorite cake and it's been passed down for generations. It was a favorite of Great Grandma Smith, who shared a birthday with my mom. So every December 3rd, her mom would make it for her.

When I was growing up, Mom always made it for us on Valentine's Day, baking the layers in heart-shaped pans to make it special. Then when I went to college, she adapted the recipe to make cupcakes and sent them to me in the mail. And these days, it is the cake my kids request every year on their birthdays.

Every time I bite into a piece, I think of my mom and how she is intentional with everything she does, and how she loves and cares for me and my family so faithfully. My mom is one of my absolute best friends. She is kind and gentle and wise and strong. A prayer warrior, so selfless and sacrificial and fun! I hope that when you bite into this cake, you will feel my mom's love being shared with you too.

CAKE

1 (15.25-ounce) package white cake mix, plus 3 tablespoons flour (see Notes for gluten-free option)

1 (3-ounce) package strawberry Jell-O instant gelatin mix (dry powder)

4 large eggs

1 cup canola oil (see Notes)

⅔ cup mashed hulled fresh strawberries (see Notes)

½ cup water

You can use either two 9-inch cake pans or three 8-inch cake pans. Line the bottom of each pan with parchment paper (trace the bottom of the cake pan on the parchment, cut it out, and place in the cake pan). Preheat the oven to 325°F if you have darker metal or nonstick pans, or to 350°F for glass or shiny metal pans.

For the cake: In a large bowl, combine all the ingredients until moistened, then beat with an electric mixer for 2 minutes on medium speed. Divide the batter evenly among the prepared cake pans.

For 9-inch pans, bake for 23 to 28 minutes; for 8-inch pans, bake for 20 to 25 minutes. (I bake the layers in my nonstick 9-inch pans at 325°F for 26 minutes.) Don't overbake: The cake is done when a toothpick inserted in the center comes out clean; the cake may look slightly browned around the edges but the top should be mostly pink. Remove the cakes from the oven and let sit for 10 minutes. Carefully run a knife around the edges and turn out the layers onto cooling racks. Let cool before assembling and frosting.

(continued)

FROSTING

½ cup unsalted butter (1 stick), slightly softened

4¼ cups powdered sugar

⅓ cup mashed hulled fresh strawberries (see Notes)

For the frosting: Beat the butter, powdered sugar, and mashed strawberries with the electric mixer until smooth. I usually chill the frosting for about 10 minutes, as it sometimes is a bit soft, and then gently stir before assembling and frosting the layers.

NOTES: For a gluten-free cake, I use a 22-ounce package of King Arthur gluten-free yellow cake mix (made for two layers) and 3 tablespoons King Arthur gluten-free "measure for measure" flour. Add all cake ingredients together and mix together with electric mixer just until mixed well. Otherwise, follow instructions as above.

For a healthier option: Instead of canola oil, use organic coconut oil made for baking and high-heat cooking (not the kind that solidifies when cold), or organic SunCoco, a sunflower oil and coconut oil blend that's made for high-heat cooking and baking.

You'll need about 12 ounces fresh strawberries to get the total of 1 cup mashed berries. You can also mash thawed frozen unsweetened strawberries instead of using fresh; you'll need about 12 ounces frozen berries.

Barb's Apple Berry Crisp

MAKES 10 SERVINGS

Who doesn't love a good berry crisp? It never goes out of season, is always loved, and can be mixed up with different berries. Plus, butter: butter makes everything absolutely delicious and comforting!

I was talking to my bestie Shan the other day and telling her I was on the hunt for a good berry crisp, when she exclaimed "Lyss, you have to try my mom's recipe. It's THE BEST!" I made it that night and let me tell you I will never try another crisp recipe. Jeff calls it "Crispalicious by Barbalicious"!

I love that it reminds me of Shannon's mom, Barb. She raised three kids who love Jesus with their whole hearts, and she always has her door open for family, friends, and neighbors to come in and be fed really good food. Last year Kinsley and I stayed at her house for a night as we were passing through their hometown, and I literally took hosting notes on how she takes care of her guests. Fluffy towels, a fresh bar of soap, books laid by the bed for Kinsley to read, coffee made before I woke up with a plethora of creamers to choose from . . . and then she packed us bento boxes of snacks for our six-hour flight home. Her hospitality—her thoughtfulness and care—touched my heart so deeply.

So, whether you want to knock your family's socks off with a delicious dessert tonight, are having some girlfriends over after dinner, or just need a little comfort food yourself, I pray you are reminded that you are loved and welcomed just as you are, in true Barb form.

4 Granny Smith apples

Juice of 1 lemon (2 tablespoons)

4 cups mixed fresh berries, as desired (see Notes)

CRUMBLE TOPPING (SEE NOTES)

1½ cups all-purpose flour (or gluten-free flour if desired)

¾ cup packed brown sugar

¾ cup granulated sugar

1 cup old-fashioned oats

1 cup (2 sticks) cold unsalted butter, diced

1 teaspoon salt

Preheat the oven to 350°F.

Peel, core, and slice the apples (like you would for an apple pie). Toss the apple slices in the lemon juice in a bowl, then spread in a 9x12-inch baking dish. Sprinkle the berries on top of the apples.

For the topping: Combine the flour, brown sugar, granulated sugar, oats, cold butter (must be cold), and salt in the bowl of an electric mixer fitted with a paddle attachment. Mix on low speed for 1 to 2 minutes, until the mixture is in large crumbles. If you don't have an electric mixer, you can use a wire whisk or your hands to mix the toppings into large crumbles. Spread the crumbles over the berries.

(continued)

Bake for 50 minutes, until berries are bubbling and topping is golden brown. Serve warm with a scoop of vanilla ice cream!

NOTES: Barb usually uses raspberries and blackberries, but you can use whatever berries you have on hand. You can also use frozen berries: Place them in a colander in the sink until defrosted, then toss with 2 tablespoons cornstarch before topping the sliced apples.

Barb usually doubles the amounts for the topping, but I like to keep them as is.

ACKNOWLEDGMENTS

To my Good Shepherd: Thank you for walking with me all the days of my life. For being my comfort and hope and best friend and Savior. All of this is for you. Thank you for letting me share my story. May it bring others close to your heart. You truly are so very good.

To my husband and best friend, Jeff: Thank you for constantly cheering me on and reminding me of God's truth over me—of his banner of love over me. You constantly teach me so much about Jesus and life and living for him. Tears always well up in my eyes when I think of how God gave you to me. This book would not be here without you. Thank you for always encouraging me to live out my giftings and follow him, no matter how scary or unknown.

To my three sweet blessings—Kinsley, Kannon, and Lucy: It is my greatest joy and honor being your mom. You truly are God's gifts to me. Thank you for making life fun and exciting, and also for pushing me to rely on Jesus every day. You are made for such a time as this. I can't wait to see how you shine your light for him, in your own unique ways.

To my mom and dad: Thank you to the ones who always said I'd be a writer. You have prayed for me, cheered me on, processed with me, and helped me fulfill this dream. Dad, thank you for showing me that true satisfaction is found only in the Lord. Mom, you are one of the greatest blessings in my life. You have faithfully walked by my side, and taught me to know and love the true King and Savior, and to savor his word. You have persevered through life's trials, clinging to Jesus, and have the most gentle and compassionate spirit I know. I hope to be as intentional, giving and loving a Mimi as you are one day.

To my dearest friends: Thank you for doing life with me, for being warrior women alongside me, for fighting the good fight of faith with me. You constantly show me Jesus' love, preach truth to my heart, and usher me to abide in his presence. I would not be the woman I am today without each one of you. Thank you, Jenna, for taking such wonderful pictures that truly bring this book to life! Thank you, Leslie, for being the first person to read my manuscript and encourage me and help me have a renewed vision for it when I had lost hope. Your support helped me to start again. Thank you, Shannon, for being my biggest cheerleader—for always cheering me on to do what God has called me to do. Thank you, Jess and Sarah, for constantly pointing me to Jesus, and walking with me in the deepest valleys. Thank you, Bianca, for being the biggest supporter and encourager. Thank you, Emilie, for listening to all my raw voxes and sharpening me to know, trust, and love Jesus more. If only I had fifty thousand more words to write down the stories of how all of you have shown me his love and spurred me on to healing, wholeness, and holiness. I hold you forever in my heart.

To Karen and Curtis Yates: You guys make our dreams come true! Thank you for being my cheerleaders, protectors, and advocates. You guys are true friends, as well as such wise counselors. Thank you for constantly being available, sharing your thoughts, guiding me, and being honest, as well as caring for my heart in the midst of it all. I am so grateful for you, and so humbled to be on your team.

To Jeana, Patsy, Katie, Laini, Rudy, Daisy, and Morgan: Every time I come away from a meeting with you guys, I have tears in my eyes because I'm so touched by your support and encouragement. Every meeting is a joy—where there is honesty and grace and a seeking to understand one another. I am so touched by how you cheer me on and work so hard to bring my ideas to life. This book would be nothing if it weren't for you guys—for your excitement, hard work, design, and grace to keep digging deeper to have it be the best it could be. It is the greatest honor to be on your team.

Angela: Friend! I truly could not have done this without you! It takes a village to make a book come to life, but it also takes a friend to walk through the depths with you. You held me up when I felt like I could go no further. You encouraged me and cheered me on when I felt like I was going crazy and wondered "Is this even good at all?!" And then you helped lift me up all over again when I needed to rewrite. You knew this book better than I did for a while! Thank you for cheering me on, for walking by my side, and for helping to give structure, flow, and clarity to my manuscript. You are such a gift to me!

ABOUT THE AUTHOR

ALYSSA JOY BETHKE has three fun and sweet kids, Kinsley, Kannon, and Lucy, and a yellow Lab, Aslan, who keep her laughing and praying each day!

She and her husband, Jeff Bethke, live in Maui and are bloggers, YouTubers, and hosts of *The Real-Life* podcast. Jeff and Alyssa are the *New York Times* best-selling authors of *Jesus > Religion* and *It's Not What You Think* and *Love That Lasts*. They are passionate about encouraging and strengthening families at familyteams.com.